THE "HUMMING BIRD"
A SMALL SEPARATOR WITH CAPACITY EQUAL TO THE LARGEST

"Russell Gearless Wind Stacker"

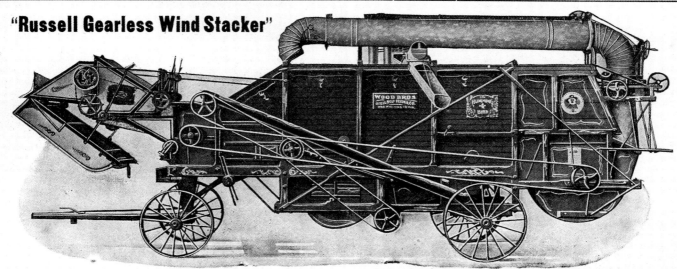

New Virginia, Iowa, 1-20-08

Wood Bros. Steel Self Feeder Co., Des Moines, Iowa.

Gentlemen:—I have been out threshing clover and got snowed under. Threshed the day that it snowed all day. The belt got wet but it stayed on and the Humming Bird stayed right with it, and it run as nice as if it had been in a bunch of flowers, and the little feeder would make the snow just fly, and the Humming Bird eat it up just like a lion. Since I have finished threshing snow and clover, I think your separator has got the wrong name. I never saw anything that would hold a candle to the Humming Bird. It has got lots of friends here and making more. Just write to Mr. Harry Lyons at New Virginia, Ia. Mr. Lyons is the hardest man that I have got to suit in Squaw Township, and you just bet the Humming Bird put him on the fence just like an owl, he could not see any grain going over in the straw or riddle, and that just suited him. You have the finest little separator on wheels. Has all kinds of capacity to thresh fast and save the grain. The shoe handles all kinds of grain and seeds in splendid shape. It is the best all round separator that I have ever run or seen run in my experience as thresherman.

G. F. MOYER.

WOOD BROTHERS STEEL SELF FEEDER COMPANY, Des Moines, Iowa

— BRANCHES —

Kansas City, Mo., Union Avenue and Hickory
Minneapolis, Minn., 226 1st Street North

St. Louis, Mo., 113 Market Street
Lincoln, Nebraska

Indianapolis, Ind., Room 6 Bd. of Trade Bldg.
Fargo, North Dakota

Motorbooks International

FARM TRACTOR COLOR HISTORY

Threshers

Text by Robert N. Pripps
Photography by Andrew Morland

To Steven, my number one son

First published in 1992 by Motorbooks International Publishers & Wholesalers, PO Box 2, 729 Prospect Avenue, Osceola, WI 54020 USA

Library of Congress
Cataloging-in-Publication Data
Pripps, Robert N.
   Threshers/Robert N. Pripps, Andrew Morland.
      p.   cm.
   Includes bibliographical references (p.   ) and index.
   ISBN 0-87938-617-7
   1. Threshing machines—History. I. Morland, Andrew. II. Title.
S699.P82 1992
633.1'045—dc20   91-40037

Printed and bound in Singapore by PH Productions

On the front cover: *A 1945 Oliver Red River Special 22 x 36 thresher at work at the 1991 Northern Illinois Steam Power Club's Sycamore Show. The Red River Special boasted ball bearings on the cylinders and all-steel construction.*

On the frontispiece: *In 1908, the Wood Bros. thresher was still made of wood, as the name of the company implies. The feeder was made of steel. Ford acquired Wood Brothers in 1941.*

On the title page: *Palmer Fossum of Northfield, Minnesota, runs his 1941 Wood Bros. Hummingbird thresher. Hooked up to a flatbelt run off of a 1946 Ford 2N tractor, the Hummingbird sang as it worked.*

Our thanks to Bud Canfield, an experienced thresherman and storehouse of threshing lore.

Peder Bjere, archivist for Varity Corporation, who provided much help with background information and for providing the Massey-Harris historical book, *Harvest Triumphant,* by Merrill Denison.

Michael Dregni, editor, Motorbooks International, whose idea it was for a book on threshers.

The Smithsonian Institution and Historical Picture Service, Chicago, for finding and providing the old pictures.

Avery Stevens, St. Charles, Illinois; Jim Polacek, Phillips, Wisconsin; and Palmer Fossum, Northfield, Minnesota, for setting up private threshings for photographer Andrew Morland.

Contents

Introduction

Thrashin' Day

thresh vb [alter. of thrash], L ter-
ere, to rub: to separate seed from a
harvested plant by mechanical
means or by beating.

—Webster

When I was a lad, my maternal grandfather had a big Case steam engine and a Case thresher, which he called a "separator." He lived in a neighborhood of small farms in north-central Wisconsin, most of which were owned by relatives. I'll never forget the excitement of threshing time: the rumbling sound of the steam engine, the lineup of horsedrawn wagons, the women bustling to prepare large meals, and the hot, dry August days. To a growing boy, threshing time compared favorably to the Christmas season.

Children would be up with the chickens on "Thrashin' Day"; Grandpa and Grandma had been up long before. Farm life in those days always began before sunup, but this day called for extra effort on everyone's part. The youngsters had to do extra morning chores so that Grandpa and Uncle Leroy could get "Old Sal," the steam engine, fired up. That meant getting the cows in and fed and milked, the eggs gathered, and the chickens fed. We also had to get the windmill hooked to the pump so that the big tank by the barn would be full for both the horses and for Old Sal, a machine with a voracious appetite for water.

Some of the older cousins were detailed to catch four or five designated

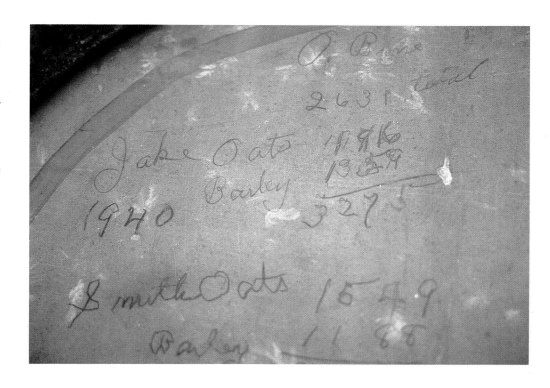

Previous page
A steam threshing outfit in Russell County, Kansas, in 1910. Note the average size crew of twelve men and a boy.

Threshing records are shown penciled on the side of a thresher from the year 1940. Threshing averaged about three cents per bushel in those days. Settlement of the charges was usually made at the end of the year, after the cash crops were sold and money received. Bernice D. Lohmeier

chickens for butchering, followed by scalding, picking, and singeing to remove the pin feathers. Others of us would build a roaring fire in Grandma's great iron stove, because Grandma—who had been up since 3 o'clock—had potatoes peeled and ready for the kettle, and ten or twelve pies ready for baking whenever the oven was hot. She wanted to get most of the baking and cooking done before the August sun made the kitchen too hot for all except the really strong.

Neighborhood threshing was an integral part of life in the Midwest then. Farms were mostly small—80 to 120 acres—which meant that owning a large, expensive piece of machinery such as a thresher was generally impractical for an individual. Therefore, such machines were often owned by as many as ten neighbors. If an individual, such as my grandfather, did own one, there was a tacit agreement with other farmers in the area that they would support it with both economic use and the manpower to operate it.

Operating a big threshing machine required about twenty-five men and boys and fifteen teams of horses with wagons if the grain shocks were still in the fields. Stack threshing required a somewhat smaller crew, but even then if the haul to the granary was long, extra help would be needed. Once the steam was up and the flatbelt was singing and the machinery was humming, woe betide if there were not enough bundles of grain to fill the maw of the thresher; enough bundles had to go in to keep the steam engine's governor open because no one wanted to hear that engine loafing.

At about 9 o'clock after finishing their own morning chores, the neighbors would begin arriving with their wagons and teams, or in their Model A Fords. It didn't pay to get started too early, as the morning dew had to be dried off before we could start. Some of the wives and daughters would come as well, bringing special dishes for the noon meal and to help Grandma with the preparations.

By then, Leroy had the separator spotted and Old Sal belted up. We kids had spent the previous weeks searching out pine knots from decaying logs and stumps in the farm's woodland. These were now the fuel for the big steamer.

As soon as the first flatbed wagons were back from the field with bundles, Leroy had the rig churning—and Old Sal was chuckling.

Grandpa would always climb on top of the rig, oilcan in hand, to supervise the operation. The older cousins usually bagged the grain and heaved the bags onto a wagon; sometimes, though, the grain was augured directly into a bin wagon. My job, as long as Grandpa had the outfit (he donated Old Sal for scrap iron during World War II), was to carry drinking water for the men and older boys in the field pitching bundles onto the wagons. This was a full-time job!

At noon, Leroy would give one long hard blast on the steam whistle to announce dinnertime. The whistle not only signaled the workers in the field, but also warned the kitchen crew.

Several washtubs of sun-warmed water stood on stands under the trees in the yard. The field crew would line up before the tubs, taking their turns scooping great handfuls of water over their heads and letting it run down their necks. This not only cleaned and cooled them, but also helped to somewhat soften the chaff caught under their shirts. A stack of cotton towels was handy. Grandma saved those too worn out for use in the kitchen for just this occasion, fearing machinery grease would ruin her good ones.

The meal, of course, was the high point of the day! Feeding the threshers was a point of competitive pride among the farm women of the era. The farmer whose wife was a good cook had no trouble getting the help he needed at threshing time.

As the men trooped from the wash stands to the dining table (planks set up on sawhorses outside), tantalizing aromas of hot bakery goods and roasting meats would greet their nostrils. Boys who were old enough to help shared in the noon repast with the men; younger boys ate with the women and girls after we were back at work.

As the family patriarch, Grandpa would offer a short blessing that included thanks for the harvest and then said, "Dig in, boys, it's not gettin' any better settin' there."

Now began a relatively quiet period while plates were loaded and dishes

were passed. The women worked behind our backs, pouring lemonade and a reddish drink called "nectar." As the first servings were consumed, conversation began: "Dewey, pass those radishes down this way, or is that your private dish?" "Earl, hand me a piece of that-there fried chicken. No, not the whole plate, just hand me a piece."

Once the peril of imminent starvation was no longer of concern the talk log jam was broken. The focal point of the camaraderie was the repartee with the meal, and there were several subjects that had to be ritually dealt with:

The heat—"Leroy, you don't need to keep throwing wood into that engine. Just open the doors and let the breeze blow through the tubes."

The wind—"Ya' know, if that wind ever quit, I think all the buildings would fall over."

The dryness—"I got a letter from my brother in Minnesota and the stamp wuz pinned on!"

The engine—"Heard about a guy over in Butternut got hisself one of them new Farmalls. He's going to use it to drive his thresher. Bet he has trouble. You just can't beat a steam engine!"

Then would come horror stories of mechanical breakdowns befalling threshers, just when they got their turn with the thresher and had all of their help ready. From there, the talk turned to other calamities, such as tales of when the food was all prepared and delay kept the threshers from showing up. In those days, there was not much in the way of refrigeration and a day's delay could be a catastrophe. You could count on a story about the lady in the Catholic community who expected to feed the threshers on Thursday, only to have the schedule slip to Friday. That meant frantically canning the beef and pork and running to town for fish.

From there, the conversation would turn to the various thresher meals they've experienced, and the relative merits of the cooks. By this time, the women were bringing in the pies, without much discretion about eavesdropping, so the subject would be quickly dropped.

After the meal, we would all sit around on the grass in the shade for about fifteen minutes, and then head back to our duties. Work continued until the farm was threshed. Generally, that would be until 4 or 5 o'clock. The neighbors would then go home for evening chores and supper.

Grandpa and Uncle Leroy would sometimes move Old Sal and the separator to the next farm before dark, and then come back to do the chores. All in all, it was quite a day! Grandpa, Leroy, and some of the older cousins would repeat it the next day, and indeed, for a week or two—starting at one end of the neighborhood one year, and the other the next. Each day, different; each day, the same. But it was harvest time, the time they had worked for all year. It was payday, so it was never boring.

Sometime between Christmas and New Year's Day, there would be a neighborhood gathering, usually at Grandpa's, for the "Day of Reckoning." It was at this time that the neighbors tallied and settled up, by cash or barter, for the year's borrowed machinery and help, all in a spirit of cooperation and goodwill. Grandpa was compensated for his threshing rig time. The feeling of camaraderie would still be prevalent on that cold winter's day as they reminisced over the excitement and good times the past threshing season.

The terms "thresh" or "threshing" have little meaning to today's younger generation, as this process now takes place in a machine called a combine. But, it used to be a labor-intensive process. From the middle of the twentieth century back to the first harvests, the process called for increasing percentages of the population to be involved. It is estimated that in the middle of the nineteenth century, 80 percent of the world's peoples spent their time producing food. In biblical times, 95 percent of the people produced food for themselves and for the other 5 percent.

What made the difference? The Industrial Revolution, the hundred-year period beginning in about 1760, started the real switch from subsistence living to specialization. More people began working in factories, which meant that fewer were left to work in food production. This more or less forced the invention of labor-saving farm machinery, such as mowers, reapers, and, finally, the threshing machine.

A steam threshing outfit in full operation. This photo was taken in 1909.

Along with the threshing machine came a new cultural phenomena called "threshing time." In addition to getting the grain harvested, this combined the camaraderie of working and eating with neighbors and the satisfaction of entering into a mutually dependent relationship with them.

By the 1950s, nearly all this had passed from the scene, as even the smaller farmers were owning their own combine machines. Gone is that sense of interdependence, replaced by independence: the ability to harvest at your own pace and schedule, with your own machine and without much of a requirement for hiring or borrowing help. Granted, this is much more efficient, but those who lived through the former times recognize that something important to society will be lost, unless preserved by restoring and maintaining the big threshing machines and by demonstrating not only their function but also the nature of the times.

My aim with this book is to give honor to this institution of rural America: threshing time. It should take its place with the corn husking bees and barn raisings. I also want to give credit to the hearty souls who keep this institution alive, those who with loving patience keep the giant machines in operating condition from year to year, just so the rest of us can attend some of the many steam and threshing shows around America. Perhaps we can catch that spirit of cooperation and camaraderie that helped make America the world's bread basket.

This, then, is the story of these big machines and of the men who designed them, and of those who now keep them as a living testimony to a way of life.

Robert N. Pripps

The Roots of Grain Harvesting

Dill is not threshed with a threshing sledge,
nor does a cart roll over cummin;
but dill is beaten out with a stick,
and cummin with a rod.

—Isaiah 28:27

In most large museums can be seen the primitive tools used for harvesting grain in such places as Egypt, Greece, and China, 2,000 years before the birth of Christ. If the museum is a complete one, you will also see European and American sickles, scythes, and harvesting tools from the beginning of the eighteenth century. The difference between the two periods is scarcely recognizable. It is a mystery to many scholars that when the planting and harvesting of crops was basic to the first man, why did he not turn his creativity to the improvement of his tools for such a long time?

Certainly, the need for improved tools was always there; reports of famine are in the earliest of recorded history. The biblical book of Ruth, written in the year 1100 B.C., describes a famine in the land of Israel and the hardships it imposed. It also gives a good description of the harvest scene of that time.

This chapter covers the development of harvesting tools, and describes how, after the reaper was invented in the 1830s, such improved tools literally forced the development of the threshing machine.

The Cradle and Flail

The first grain that was raised was probably stripped from the stalk by

Previous page
The McCormick reaper at work in a field, circa 1831. The machine could cut eight or nine acres per day, if conditions were good. Besides a man to drive the horse and one to rake the grain off the platform, the job required four or five hand binders to bind and stack the bundles. International Harvester

The Marsh harvester, circa 1858, pioneered the use of a conveyor to transport the cut grain over the right wheel the bundler could ride. This feature facilitated the invention of the automatic binder, because there was now room to put it, without turning the grain. The harvester-binder increased productivity to the point where development of the thresher was driven to keep up. Historical Pictures Service, Chicago

The Gallic header, a first-century attempt at perfecting a reaping machine. The cart was pushed into standing grain; metal "fingers" at the leading edge supposedly caught the stalks and stripped off the heads, which then fell back into the box of the cart.

hand without the plant being cut. Besides being a tedious process, this was also a wasteful one, and left the long straw in the way to hamper further planting. The first harvesting tool to be invented was the reaping hook, or sickle. The earliest of these were wooden, and although sharpened to the greatest extent possible, required much effort to swing, especially given the awkward operating position necessary with all sickle cutting.

The advent of primitive metallurgy saw sickles as among the first tools to be converted. The main result was an easier swing through the standing grain. As time progressed, the curve of the sickle was straightened, the blade lengthened, and a stand-up handle, or "snath," added. The scythe was born.

Now, two hands could be used to swing the blade through the stalks, and production rose from less than an acre per day to almost four. The harvester was now released from the symbolic stoop of serfdom, which had been his lot since the beginning of grain harvesting. With his head held high and his arms and body swinging in a natural motion, the work became easier.

In the late 1700s, the European Quakers produced another

improvement in the scythe: the cradle scythe, or cradle. The cradle had wooden "fingers," or rods, behind the blade and attached to the blade and handle to form a basket-like arrangement. As the "reaper," as such field hands were called, swung the blade through the grain, the cradle caught and held the severed stalks. When the reaper brought his blade back for the next swing, the gavel, or bunch of loose grain, was deposited on the ground behind him. There it waited for the bandster to bind it into sheaves.

The real significance of the cradle is that it was the first combine. It was the first farm tool invention that combined two functions: that of the cutter and the raker. The cradle was the apex of hand tool development. With it, one man and a helper could reap, bind, and stack more than five acres between sunup and sundown of a long, hot summer day.

The procedures for processing the grain after it was cut also evolved over the centuries. Until the mid-nineteenth century, however, the process usually included an enclosed area known as a threshing floor. It was here that the grain was separated from the stalks and de-hulled. Originally, this was accomplished either by beating the grain with a stick or club, or by walking sharp-footed animals over it as it lay on the threshing floor.

It is not known just when the flail was invented, but surely it also goes back to the earliest recordings. The flail consists of a short wooden club attached to a long wooden handle with a leather joint. The long handle enabled the thresher to stand upright as he lashed the grain spread out on the threshing floor. The club, or "swiple," ruptured the hulls and separated the grain from the stalks and chaff. Wielding the flail took much practice before one could efficiently thresh grain. The beginner took a considerable beating about the head and shoulders.

New England colonial farmers perfected the flail and used it to good advantage. But the flail was not unique to Western culture; early Japanese records show it being used singly or in conjunction with a comb-type of stripper called a "mogi-kogi."

The job of threshing was often left for the winter months, when the outside work was done or when the fields became too wet or frozen for further tillage. Cold, dry weather was best for threshing because, if the grain was damp, it would not come out of the heads. Once the grain was out of the hulls, the straw was raked away and the grain and hull chaff were swept up for further processing. On the average, one good flail thresher could process seven bushels of wheat, eighteen bushels of

The cradle was the most efficient means of cutting grain before McCormick's invention of the reaper. As the operator swung the blade through the standing grain, it fell back on the frame of wooden fingers. On the backswing, it would drop off in a relatively straight row. A bundler could go to work on it directly, eliminating the need for a raker.
International Harvester

A patent model of a flail-type threshing machine. Several units of this approach to threshing were tried on both sides of the Atlantic, as early inventors simply tried to mechanize the job of flail threshing.

oats, fifteen bushels of barley, or eight bushels of rye in a day.

Sledge Threshing

As farmers began to specialize and grow the types of crops that best grew in their areas, competition for labor drove them to labor-saving shortcuts. The first of these was walking animals, such as oxen, horses, or donkeys, over

Cradle scythe, attached to the wall at the Deere & Company World Headquarters in Moline, Illinois. The cradle was the first farm tool to combine two functions: that of cutting (formerly done by the scythe) and piling (formerly done by the raker). With his foreswing, the reaper, as such fieldhands were called, cut the grain stalks off near the ground. The stalks fell back and lay evenly upon the wooden rack behind the blade. As the reaper swung to the top of his forestroke, the grain stalks dropped off onto the ground in a neat pile ready for the bandster to tie it into bundles.

A threshing sledge shown hanging on the wall at the Deere & Company World Headquarters in Moline, Illinois. This toboggan-like affair was pulled by animal power around the threshing floor over grain bundles spread thereon. The farmer would ride standing on the rig to give it weight. Note the pock-marks in the bottom of the sledge; stones were embedded in these indentations (some are still present) to give teeth to the machine.

A riddle (screen) and a homemade thresher on display at the Deere & Company World Headquarters in Moline, Illinois. The riddle was used to separate grain from straw and chaff after it had been threshed with a sledge, flail, or primitive threshing machine, such as the one shown. Grain, straw, chaff,

and other debris were scooped up from the threshing floor and dumped into the riddle. The riddle was then heaved up and down so that the contents would be tossed into the air and caught again. The screen was sized so that kernels of grain would pass through, and all else would remain in the riddle.

the stalks of grain on the threshing floor to separate the grain from the hulls and stalks. This was called treading out the grain.

Treading was substantially faster than threshing by flail. One or two men and three horses could tread out about thirty bushels in a twelve-hour day. The process called for several bundles of grain to be spread out in a circle; the animals, tied in the middle of the

15

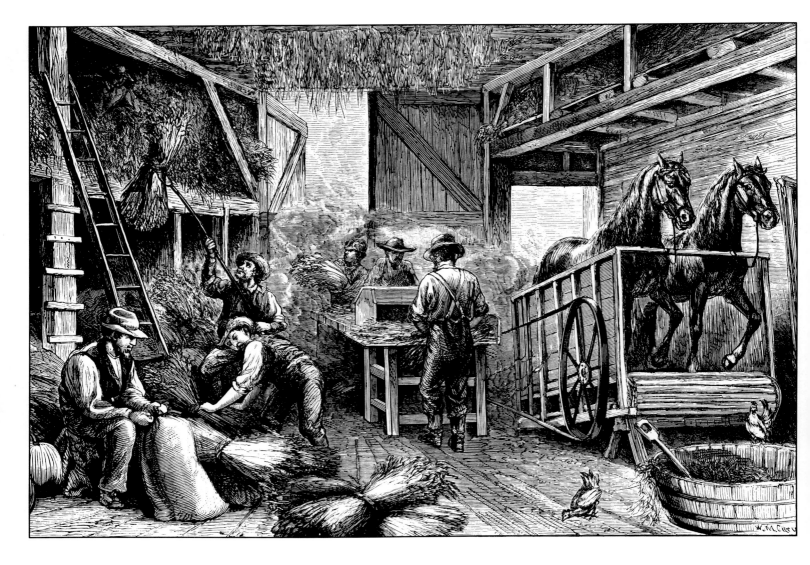

Barn threshing, circa 1850. Originally, non-portable threshing machines were set up on the threshing floor in the barn. As the grain was harvested, it was brought in from the fields and stacked in the barn. Threshing was then done in the winter months, as time permitted. Historical Pictures Service, Chicago

threshing floor, were walked around the circle over the grain. To get as much grain as possible in contact with the hoofs, the straw was frequently turned with a fork.

Treading was not nearly as efficient as flail threshing, however, because despite the efforts of the farmer to turn and shift the straw, the animals' hoofs still missed a lot of the grain heads. Nevertheless, farmers with many acres

to harvest found treading more economical than flailing.

In an effort to improve upon the efficiency of animal threshing and to exceed the speed capability of flailing, farmers advanced to sledge threshing. The ancient Egyptians had a device called a "charatz," which was something like the "stone boat" used on farms in America, into which stones from the fields were gathered for transport to the place where they could be dumped. The charatz was intentionally made rough on the bottom. The Romans used a similar toboggan-like device called a "tribulum." At about the same time, the Hebrews perfected a device called a "moreg." The moreg had sled-like runners, between which rollers with spikes were placed. The sledge, of whatever type, was then hauled around

the threshing floor by sharp-footed animals, while the farmer forked, turned, raked, and swept.

Sledge threshing is still used in underdeveloped countries. It is more efficient than treading, but not much faster.

Winnowing and the Fanning Mill

Once the grain had been flailed, trampled, or sledged from the ears, the straw was raked away and the grain and chaff were swept into a pile for cleaning. In the early days, cleaning was done by winnowing the grain from the chaff.

There were several winnowing methods. The first used a wide, shallow basket to toss the grain and chaff into the air. The breeze blew the chaff and

16

BELL'S REAPING MACHING PUT IN OPERATION IN 1828.

A. Apron which receives the grain.   B   Tongue to which the horses were attached   W   Reel   T   Cutter

Patrick Bell's reaping machine, although a forerunner to the McCormick machine, did not see production on any considerable scale and never saw the development that was afforded McCormick's. It did have one important feature that, at least in theory, was ahead of its time; it was self-raking. Unlike the McCormick machine, it was pushed, rather than pulled, by the horses.

dust away, while the grain fell back into the basket. The winnower continued the tossing until as much chaff as possible had been removed.

A second winnowing method involved pouring the grain and chaff from one container to another and letting the breeze carry it away during the fall, as before. To speed up the process, a device called a "riddle" was sometimes used.

This was simply a sieve or screen that separated the larger pieces of chaff. Riddling was also done in the breeze so that chaff passing through the screen would be carried away from the grain.

Winnowing grain remained a common practice well into the nineteenth century. The lack of a breeze was sometimes overcome by waving a sheet of cloth to create a wind. This

17

Threshing Machines in Great Britain

The British claim that the first working threshing machine in the world was built by Andrew Meikle in Scotland in 1786. His machines were popular on the big farms of the Scottish Lowlands where labor was scarce. The machines were installed in barns and driven by horses or by water power.

The design of machines developed quickly in the early 1800s. The beating of the crop gave way to rubbing and winnowing fans, which separated the grain from the chaff. The mechanization of farming was causing unemployment for many farm workers whose families had worked on the land for generations. In southern England, hundreds of threshing machines were attacked and set on fire because the use of threshing machines was resented.

In 1833, when six agricultural workers in Tolpuddle, Dorset, formed a trade union to defend their jobs and get better pay, they were transported to Australia.

In the 1850s, threshing machines became portable and a large number were used by contractors, who went from farm to farm in southern England.

The British threshing machine was nearly always hand-fed. The early machines being dangerous, the later machines made it more difficult to feed your arms and hands into the drum. The hand-fed system was less wasteful with the crop, which was more valuable in England than in the United States. Even in the late forties, British threshing machines did not use the American conveyer system.

---

artificial airflow proved so desirable that it led to the invention of the fanning mill.

Around the turn of the nineteenth century, British farmers were already cleaning with the fanning mill. It consisted of a box-like structure that contained several screens and housed a series of wooden paddles attached to an axle. The axle was usually driven via gears or chain and sprockets from a hand crank. Grain and chaff were poured into the top of the box while the crank was turned. The rapidly moving paddles drew air into the box through openings in the side and expelled it through the screens and out the exit. The grain fell through the screens to the bottom of the box, and the chaff was carried out by the airflow.

Fanning mill operation usually required three persons: one to pour in the uncleaned grain, one to turn the crank, and one to scoop the cleaned grain from the bottom of the box into a basket and sack it and then stack the bags.

Some fanning mills required more than one operator, and some were adapted to horsepower. The common one-man machine could clean about 500 bushels in a day. This included time for running the grain through twice to assure thorough cleaning.

By 1840, the fanning mill had completely replaced winnowing, and remained a useful tool into the twentieth century, as early threshing machines did not have blowers. Many farmers also used the fanning mill to clean their seed before planting with a grain drill. Clean seed caused much less clogging and resulted in more even planting.

The Reaper

As early as the first century A.D., there were attempts to mechanize the task of collecting, or reaping, grain. These early efforts took the form of head-strippers. The device was usually a box on wheels or runners, pushed by oxen into the standing grain. The leading upper edge of the box was a metal bar with sharp, tapered slots. As the contraption advanced, the stalks entered the slots and the "ears" were stripped and fell into the box behind. At least that is what happened in theory. The fact that these stripping harvesters did little to replace the scythe, or even the reaping hook, is testimony to their inefficiency.

Nevertheless, in 1783, the British Royal Society of Arts, Manufacturers and Commerce published a 100-year-old report written by a Roman author, describing such strippers and calling them successful. To its publication of the report, the Society added the challenge of a prize to the inventor of the first successful reaping machine.

Over the next fifteen or twenty years, many enterprising men undertook the challenge, but without success. Their attempts took the approach that a mechanical reaper should duplicate the motion of a human reaper. Needless to say, in this time frame, such complicated mechanisms were problematical. An Englishman by the name of Salmon did, however, invent a mowing machine that used two serrated cutting bars, one on top of the other, which oscillated in opposite directions. Also used were projecting fingers in front of the cutter bars, to hold the stalks against the cutters, and a "divider" bar, which separated the stand to be cut from that to be left for the next pass.

The importance of Salmon's invention was missed, however, for the Society saw it as a cutter, but not the reaper for which the prize was offered. Ironically, Salmon's cutter bar design is still basic to grain harvesters today.

In 1823, Englishman Henry Ogle began to produce and sell devices patterned after the Salmon machine, but to which were added the now familiar sweep reel. The Ogle reaper was said to be able to harvest about fourteen acres per day. Four years later, another Englishman, Patrick Bell, developed a similar device, except that where the Ogle reaper was pulled, the Bell machine was pushed.

On the American side of the Atlantic, efforts were also underway to perfect a reaping machine. One such inventor was Robert McCormick, father of Cyrus Hall McCormick. Robert succeeded, as did his British counterparts, in making a workable grain cutter, but it, too, left the grain stalks too tangled for binding. Son Cyrus was no doubt party to these endeavors as he was growing up. Then, in July 1831, Cyrus Hall McCormick, having picked up where his father left off, demonstrated the first truly successful reaping machine.

An early Pope thresher, circa 1930. This unit could have been turned by a hand crank or by a one-horse horse-powered treadmill. It did not use a fan or any means of separating the grain and chaff, but simply deposited the whole mess under the machine. Winnowing had to be done as before. The Pope thresher did a more efficient job of loosening the kernels from the heads, however, than did some of its fancier contemporaries.

The McCormick reaper used a sickle bar fashioned after the Salmon cutter, with the fingers projecting out front to hold the stalks for cutting. It also used the divider of the Salmon machine, and its sweep reel was like that of the Ogle and Bell reapers. McCormick's reaper had several unique features, including a platform onto which the grain fell, to then be raked off onto the ground in bunches suitable for bundling; a side-mounted hitch for the horse, and hence the line of draft, thereby allowing the horse to walk in the stubble of the swath already cut, rather than trample the standing grain; and one main wheel, which operated the cutter and carried the machine, mounted directly behind the horse in the line of draft. With a McCormick reaper, two men and a horse could harvest about an acre per hour.

McCormick sold a few of his first reapers, but most farmers were not clamoring for them and considered them to be curiosities. American farms of the 1830s were not sufficiently developed to be free of stumps, humps, and rocks, and farmers were skeptical of the machine's ability to work. McCormick also found some of the reticence encountered by his British counterparts; resentful farm laborers feared that these machines would throw them out of work.

Given the lack of a market for reapers, Cyrus and Robert McCormick

An 1876 Minard Harder Fearless outfit is depicted in this engraving. Except for the lack of a feeder-cutter, this thresher represents a fairly high state of development for the time. Note that the wheels on the horse-powered treadmill could be adjusted to make the treadmill steeper, if required. Historical Pictures Service, Chicago

diverted their attention to other farm inventions and manufacturing activities, including the McCormick cast-iron plow, which sold well before the steel plow was invented. But, while their interests were elsewhere, Obed Hussey, of Nantucket, Massachusetts, secured, in 1833, the first US patent for a reaping machine.

The Hussey patent got Cyrus's attention. He immediately filed for his own patent, which was granted in 1834. Thus began a bitter conflict that lasted for years.

Hussey's reaper was somewhat different from McCormick's, in that it had two drive wheels, plus smaller wheels to carry the cutter, it used no reel, and side delivery was not provided. Consequently, the binder had to keep up with the machine for the sheaves to be out of the way before it came around again. The main advantage of the Hussey reaper was the open-top guard finger on the cutter bar. This allowed chaff and other debris to exit, instead of plugging up and jamming the cutter.

By 1840, McCormick was beginning to enter the market in earnest. The Hussey machine's popularity, because of some unfortunate changes, was beginning to wane. Feeling the pressure of competition, Hussey challenged McCormick to a field trial. By 1843, Hussey and McCormick agreed to a public contest, to be held in the James River area of Virginia. Each machine was to harvest similar plots of the same field. The first one done was the winner. Twice, McCormick's reaper finished ahead of Hussey's, because of mechanical problems with the Hussey machine and the more difficult binding situation.

Hussey continued to challenge McCormick in the field and in the courtroom until his death in 1860 in a railroad accident. Unfortunately for both men, their patents expired at just about the time that mechanical reaping was gaining wide acceptance with farmers. This was especially true when the self-raker appeared on the market.

Walter Wood, inventor of Wood's Celebrated Patent System of Harvest Machinery, did not claim that the self-raking reaper was solely his idea, but stated, "I have assimilated with my inventions, as far as was necessary, those of others, having secured them by purchase." The self-raker really was just the next logical step in the reaper's evolution: a mechanical means of eliminating the need for someone to

rake off the grain in bundles for binding. Soon, a plethora of self-raking reapers were on the market, and in the late 1850s, the reel-rake reaper was introduced by several companies.

One of the best of these reel-rake reapers was the Kirby. A similar one was developed in Canada by the Harris Company, later to be part of Massey-Harris. The reel-rake had four rakes, or elongated paddles with teeth, mounted on a semi-vertical, or tilted, shaft. The shaft, driven by the wheels, caused each paddle to sweep the table of cut stalks, then swing up over the rest of the machine and down again into the uncut grain, which it combed into the cutter bar.

The great advantage of the reel-rake was efficiency. Previously, the fields had to be raked by hand to glean the straws scattered by the reaper. This was not necessary with the reel-rake.

The success of the reaper signaled the turning point for agriculture. With the reaper, farmers required other tools that would allow them to capitalize on their newfound ability to harvest larger quantities more efficiently. Steel plows, planters, mowers, binders, threshers, and steam engines soon followed. This era saw the establishment of giants of the farm machinery business; McCormick, Deere, Case, and Massey became household words, and the

United States and Canada became food producers to the world.

The Self-Binding Harvester

To quote Merrill Denison from his book *Harvest Triumphant*, "Next to the wheel, the cutter bar and the reel, the invention that did most for agricultural mechanization was the automatic knotter, the mechanism which did away with hand labor for the tying of the sheaves. It was this amazing device that transformed the reaper into the self-binder, a machine which has exerted a more profound influence on the world's economy than any other of man's technical accomplishments, save possibly the locomotive."

Denison goes on to say that the self-binder saved 25 percent in harvesting manpower and caused a real change, in the space of two decades, in the rural-urban population split. The earliest self-binders, however, were not the giant-step that the above quote might lead one to believe.

The task of perfecting the self-raking reapers was not yet complete when the Marsh brothers, Charles and William, introduced their first harvester. Their machine conveyed the cut grain from the apron and up over the drive wheel, delivering it to a table where two men, riding on the machine, bound the grain into bundles and unloaded them. Thus, two men riding could bind as much as four men following a self-raking reaper. Hand binding was generally done with a sheaf of straw wrapped around the bundle.

The Deering Harvester Company grew out of the Marsh invention, although defects in their patents kept the Marsh Brothers from obtaining much of their deserved rewards. Nevertheless, the way was opened for the next logical step: the self-binder.

Even though a number of attempts had been made at automatic binding as early as 1850, it was not until the Marsh brothers showed the world how to convey the grain over the drive wheel that a place for the complicated binding mechanism could be found.

There were still complications, however. Early binders used wire for binding, and this introduced a whole new set of problems, such as cattle eating pieces of wire and loose pieces of wire snarling the cutter bars.

By 1868, some eighty binder patents had been issued. Cyrus McCormick stated that he considered these to be "newfangled, half-fledged contrivances, calculated to delude the farmer by representations of wonder-working powers no machine yet possesses." Nevertheless, wire binders were quite popular for about ten years. The Walter A. Wood machine of 1873 sold well and was one of the best of the wire-tie binders.

Twine was also considered, but wire-tie binders were easier to build and operate, and there were as yet only one or two twine mills in the country. Thus, twine was hard to find and was expensive when available.

John F. Appleby of DePere, Wisconsin, is credited with the first commercially successful twine binder. He began work on a wire binder in 1858, but eventually switched to twine. In 1873, his twine binder was performing well enough, but short of funds to continue, he offered it to McCormick. McCormick developers looked at it on two different occasions, but decided it was of no value to them.

Appleby next offered his invention to William Deering, one of McCormick's competitors. Deering snapped up the Appleby design, along with the rights to the Behel "knotter bill," a device for holding the twine in the knotter. With these patents available to him, Deering made some 3,000 twine binders for the harvest of 1880. The McCormick Company finally came up with a twine binder in 1884, the year of the death of Cyrus McCormick, who during his life had witnessed one of the most remarkable transformations in agricultural history.

The success of Deering's twine binder caused a severe shortage of twine, and eventually higher twine prices threatened the sales of his machines. Deering discussed the problem with a Philadelphia manufacturer by the name of Edwin Fitler. Fitler agreed to add twine manufacturing to his schedule only after Deering gave him a firm order for ten carloads of twine. Soon, other manufacturers began making twine, and the price-availability problem was over.

Twine soon became the common medium for binders, but within years the binder was replaced by the harvester, as shown in this 1936 ad for Allis-Chalmers' All-Crop harvester. The advantages were clearly listed: No twine, no shocking, no threshing, and most important of all, no extra men to feed at suppertime.

By 1902, the McCormick and Deering Companies, both giants of the harvesting industry, merged with several others to form International Harvester.

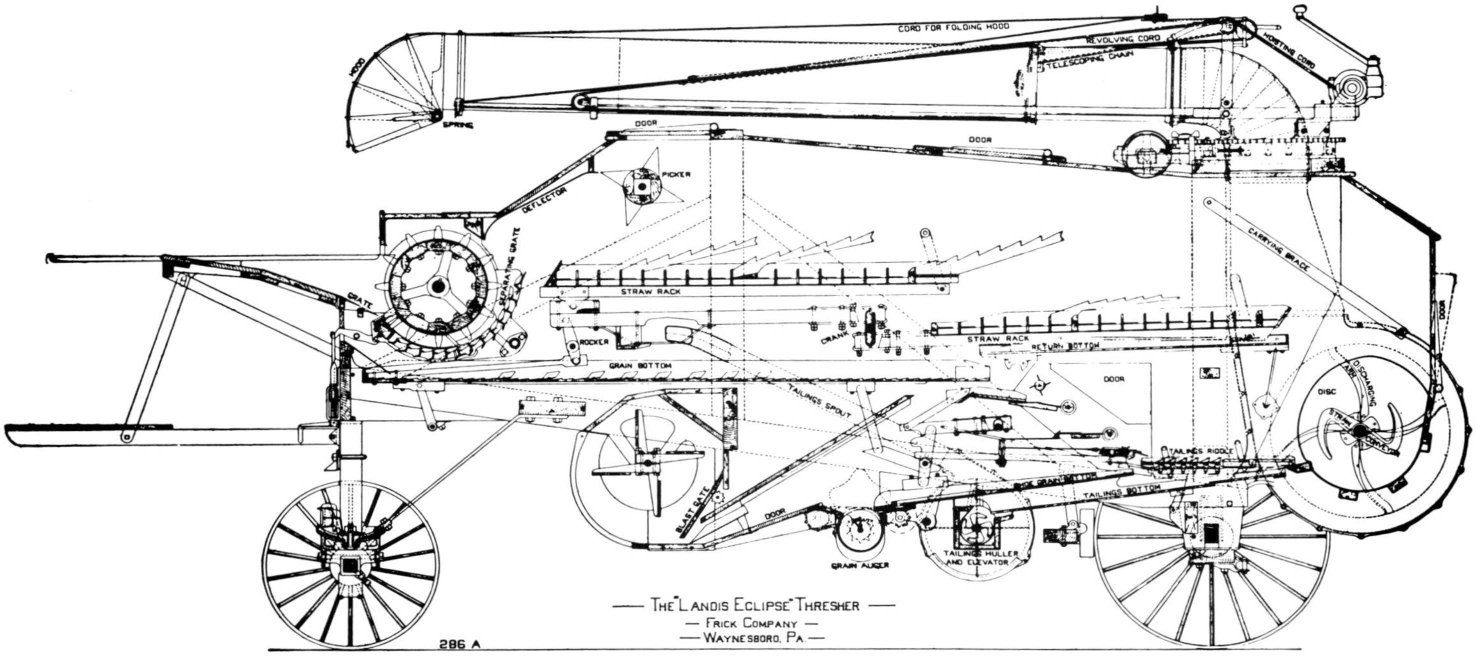

The "Landis Eclipse" Thresher—Sectional View

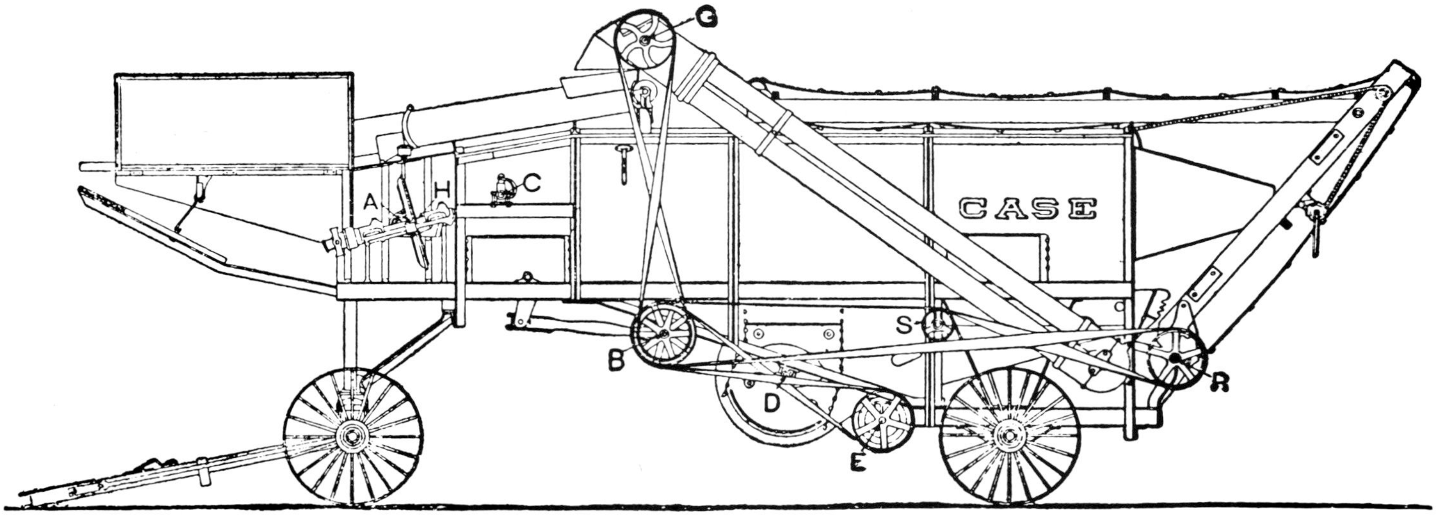

FIG. 47. RIGHT SIDE OF GEARED SEPARATOR WITH COMMON STACKER.

Number	Shaft	Diameter	Face	Bore	Name.
501T	A	8¼	8	1⅝	Main drive pulley, 36 to 42". (On belt machines.)
5904T	A	9¼	9	1⅝	Main drive pulley, 46". (On belt machines.)
5294T	A	13½	9	2 7/16	Main drive pulley, 50" and up. (On belt machines.)
1605T	B	13	3	1⅜	Pulley drives common stacker.
5158T	S	6½	3¼	1	Idler pulley.
A1677T	R	12	3¼	1 1/16	Pulley on common stacker shaft.
1673T	B	10½	2¼	1⅜	Pulley drives tailings elevator.
529T	G	13	2½	15/16	Pulley on tailings elevator shaft.
1605T	B	13	3	1⅜	Pulley drives grain auger.
1223T	E	13	2½	15/16	Pulley on grain auger shaft.
5434T	D	6½	2¼	1 15/16	Pulley drives shoe shake (50" and up).
5431T	F	8	2¼	15/16	Pulley on shoe shake shaft (50" and up).

Early Threshing Machines

Behold, I will make thee
a new sharp
threshing instrument having teeth . . .
—Isaiah 41:15

Contemplating the physical effort involved in preparing a loaf of bread at the turn of the nineteenth century is mindboggling by our standards of labor. The soil had to be turned and tilled with a primitive plow or spade, the seed had to be sown by hand, and the grain had to be cut with a sickle or scythe; then came the laborious task of threshing the grain from the stalk, followed by winnowing the chaff and straw from the grain—all before the grain could be milled into flour for baking. Yet, this was the only process until 1820, when a Bostonian by the name of John Pope popularized what eventually became known as the groundhog thresher.

Even after the threshing machine was invented, plenty of hard work was still necessary to produce a loaf of bread. Threshing machines came into being in the eighteenth century, more as a means to improve efficiency and to reduce waste than as a labor-saving device. Also, and of no small consideration, the really hard work could then be transferred from man to horse and machine.

First Patents

The earliest patent for a threshing machine seems to have been granted to Michael Menzies of Scotland, in 1732.

Previous page
A cross-section view of the Landis Eclipse thresher, by Frick Company of Waynesboro, Pennsylvania. Note this is a fairly early model which still requires hand feeding, although it uses a wind stacker.

Below, a cross-section view of a later Case Thresher.

Detail of the decal on the Robert Bell Imperial thresher.

In 1902 this machine thrashed all the wheat in five counties. And it and one other thrashed all wheat in seven counties in 1904. Mr. J. C. Wamble owner on machine

This Agitator machine was hand-fed and used a conveyor-type straw stacker. Note the thresherman is in his place atop the machine, where he can observe all aspects of the operation.

His device was simply a water-powered contraption driving a large number of flails. He claimed it could "deliver as many strokes as thirty-three men threshing briskly." Scotland may be considered the cradle of the threshing machine, as a second was also made there by a man named Leckie in 1758. The Leckie machine, while also doomed to failure, was at least a step in the right direction, because the threshing cylinder was enclosed in a concave case.

But it wasn't until 1788 when a practical threshing machine was patented, again by a Scot, Andrew Meikle. His was a water-powered device that used beating cylinders to thresh and an apron (a slatted conveyor) to clean the grain. Improvements were added over the years, and in 1800, a fanning mill was added—and at last a complete separator was available.

In 1791, Samuel Mulliken of Philadelphia, Pennsylvania, patented the first American threshing machine. Not much is known about the Mulliken machine, except that it was quite complicated and didn't work very well. Consequently, threshing machines were not generally available in America until after the War of 1812, when British machines were imported. Even then, only the largest and most prosperous farmers could afford the imports for a number of reasons other than the cost.

First, all threshing machines of the time were stationary, usually mounted in a separate building to facilitate the use of water power or the "cider mill" type of horsepower. This precluded the sharing of a threshing machine among neighboring farmers.

Second, these early machines required four to six teams of horses to power them; add to this the teams required to collect the grain bundles and to accomplish other farm activities, and it is obvious that the average farmer would not have that many horses available.

Third, these foreign machines were unreliable, and repair parts were difficult to obtain. A minor part breakage in the midst of the threshing season meant endless delay, and it was exasperating to have to hand flail and fan while the idle, expensive monster looked on.

It wasn't until the 1820s that a reliable, locally made thresher was available in the United States. This was the Pope machine, made in Boston, which was hand-powered and used an endless belt conveyor to carry the grain and straw into a spiked cylinder-concave with iron teeth. These machines didn't separate; they simply threshed. The grain and chaff came out on the ground below the machine. Separating and fanning, as before,

24

Field threshing in about 1911. The advantage of this method over barnyard threshing was that the bundles did not have to be hauled so far. As shown here, the grain is augered directly into a box wagon to be hauled to the granary. This method left the straw stack in the field, which usually meant later moving it to a more convenient location.

followed. The Pope machine was more efficient than other threshers of its time; that is, it did a better job of beating the heads from the husks and off the stalks, but providing the manpower was harder than wielding a flail. To eliminate that complaint, horsepower was soon added.

These threshers, and others that soon followed, were semi-portable. They could be hauled around by wagon and set up at the threshing site. The machine was staked to the ground, and its attendant horse-powered treadmill was dug into a pit on one end so that

the horses could walk up an incline. Thus, the angle and motion of both pieces gave the illusion of an animal digging in the ground. Threshing machines of this type soon got the popular nickname of groundhog threshers.

Pitts Brothers Thresher

Hiram and John Pitts of Winthrop, Maine, were influential in the development of the threshing machine in the middle of the nineteenth century. First, they acquired a groundhog machine and became itinerant threshers. Troubles with their horse-powered treadmill caused them to seek ways to improve this mechanism. In 1830, Hiram obtained a patent for a treadmill incorporating hard maple rollers under the treads and substituting a chain belt for the previously used leather belt.

The commercial success of these treadmills led Hiram to look further into improving their threshing

business. Over the next seven years, he and John devised many improvements, eventually making their own machine. It used the groundhog-type of open cylinder, but incorporated a fanning mill to clean the grain and a slatted, endless belt, or apron, to carry away the straw.

Grain bundles were fed into the cylinder and the grain was beaten from the heads. Grain, straw, and chaff dropped onto the apron, a riddle-like conveyer of wooden slats attached to end chains. Most of the grain fell between the slats and, as it fell to the bottom of the machine, was winnowed by the fan. The straw and chaff piled up at the end of the machine.

The Pitts brothers received a patent on their machine in 1837. Although still lacking much in efficiency and durability, the Pitts thresher was a great improvement over the original groundhog. Using a Pitts thresher, four men—one to haul bundles, one to feed the machine, one to bag the grain, and

25

A Robert Bell Imperial thresher at work at the Ontario Agricultural Museum. Bell threshers and tractors were built at the company's works in Seaforth, Ontario.

one to fork away the straw—could thresh about 100 bushels per day using two horses to power the treadmill. This was at least two times the production possible per man as with the Pope groundhog.

In addition to its productivity, the Pitts thresher was quite portable. It was small and light enough to be carried on a wagon drawn by the same two horses that powered it. Once on site, it and the treadmill could be set up and running in about thirty minutes.

The Pitts brothers manufactured their machines together until 1840,

when John pulled out and went to Albany, New York, where he joined with another manufacturing pioneer, Joseph Hall. From there, he moved his operation first to Rochester, New York, then to Springfield, Ohio, and finally to Buffalo, New York. Here, he manufactured the Buffalo Pitts threshing machine until his death in 1859.

Meanwhile, Hiram Pitts remained in Winthrop manufacturing threshers. By 1847, he saw that the market for such machines had largely moved west. Accordingly, he relocated his factory first to Alton, Illinois, and then in 1851, to Chicago. His machine became known as the Chicago Pitts thresher. Hiram's death in 1860 ended the reign of the Pitts threshers.

"The Pitts brothers invention marked a distinct era in the history of

threshing machines," according to Robert L. Audrey in his book, *American Agricultural Implements*, "and although various improvements have been made in the details of this type of thresher, it is a remarkable fact that they followed the principles covered by the original patent all the way down for more than half a century."

The problem had not been getting the grain off the straw, but separating it from the straw after it had been threshed. The approach the Pitts had taken, and that of all successive apron-type machines, is that of an ascending conveyor with unsteady motion; thus, the grain is shaken down through the straw, where it falls through the slats of the conveyor. The separation process is aided along the way by straw pickers and beaters. Little of the grain was lost by the Pitts thresher.

Top view of a horse-power with sweeps attached.

Vibrating Threshers

A contemporary of the Pitts brothers was Jacob Wemple, a blacksmith from Mineyville, New York. Frequently hired to repair threshing machines, Wemple became interested in making one of his own design. His machine differed from those of the Pitts brothers in the shape of the cylinder teeth and in the manner of fastening the teeth to the cylinder.

In 1840, Wemple entered into an agreement with George Westinghouse, father of the inventor of the air brake. Together, they devised a separator mechanism that had a more distinct vibratory motion than those of the Pitts brothers, which relied solely on the

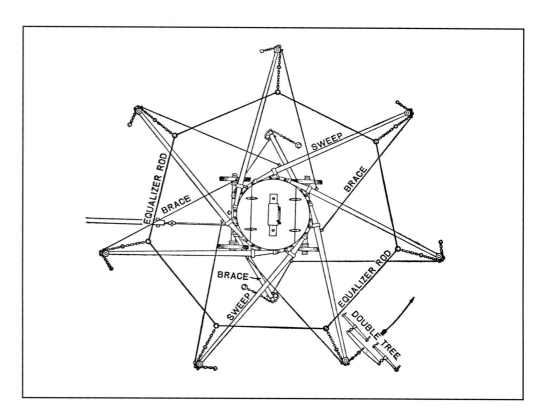

Threshers were heavy mechanisms, as were steam traction engines. The weight of this outfit was clearly too much for this bridge in Paulding County, Georgia, 1920.

jiggle of the chain drive mechanism. The Wemple-Westinghouse separator used a slotted, canvas conveyor, running on square rollers. The shaking motion fluffed the straw and shook the grain through to fall between the slots. They obtained a patent on their machine, officially known as the Wemple thresher, in 1843. Unofficially, it was known as the bull thresher for reasons historians do not agree upon (but possibly because of the roar it made when in operation).

Soon after the patent was obtained, Westinghouse left the partnership and moved to Schenectady, New York, where he continued to build the bull thresher until his death in 1844. Wemple moved to Chicago in 1848 and made the bull thresher through 1852, when he sold out to Hiram Pitts.

In the late 1840s, a pair of inventors in Belleville, Illinois, John Cox and Cyrus Roberts, began making their own version of the groundhog thresher. Instead of the slatted conveyor of the Pitts machines, they used a vibrating pan, a crank, and pitman arm connecting rods. The straw was forced along in the process and dropped off the end of the pan. This approach to separating the grain from the straw was perfected by Cox and Roberts over the next several years. They incorporated such improvements as jumping rollers on tracks to shake the pan up and down, independent of the back-and-forth motion.

By 1856, the Cox and Roberts thresher was a fairly respectable rig; it was also manufactured by Kingsland and Ferguson of St. Louis, Missouri, who helped develop the principle. Nevertheless, the full potential of the vibrator was not realized until 1858, when the Nichols & Shepard Company of Battle Creek, Michigan, took up the idea. Their first improvements were in the area of straw handling, with lifting fingers that fluffed the straw as it went along and a second shaker added below the first.

The upper shaker was the traditional perforated pan of the Cox and Roberts design, while the lower was more like the conveyor of the Westinghouse bull thresher. The lower was oscillated back and forth in opposition to the upper, thus removing vibrations otherwise transferred to the machine frame.

H. H. Taylor of Chicago, Illinois, and later, C. Aultman of Canton, Ohio, bought interests in the vibrator patents. In 1867, Aultman and Taylor merged and formed the company bearing their names in Mansfield, Ohio. With its continued development and considerable influence on the threshing machine business, the advent of the vibrating thresher numbered the days of its cousin, the apron-type thresher.

Threshing Days: I Was There

By Clyde Bearrows

It's 6 a.m., and pots and pans are rattling downstairs. Better get up; Dad's already doing the chores. Just about time for the 6:15 Burlington passenger to go through. The old engineer has her hooked up real good—a trail of black smoke a mile long. I love to watch that train go through. Its smoothness could not be equaled.

After a light breakfast of pancakes and sausage, Dad is ready to start cutting grain. Four horses on the old McCormick binder, my job was to throw the bundles out as he made the back swath. Click, click, click—out came the bundles. Once in awhile, there would be one that wasn't tied. We would always take a jug of ginger water with us when it was hot.

We always changed horses at noon. They got pretty tired when it was hot. We had a whip in the whip socket on the old binder, but to my knowledge, the whip was never used.

A couple years later, Dad bought a 15-25 Emerson-Brantingham tractor that we used to pull the binder, and by then I was promoted to ride the binder. I rode the binder from the time the dew was off the grass until nearly dark. I had a good pillow on the seat.

After the chores were done and we had supper, the moon would come out and Dad would say, "Let's go and set up a few," because by then it was cool.

When the grain had been shocked, it was time to go to more interesting things. Dad wanted to get the old Advance steam engine out, which always needed a lot of tinkering done to it. We wrapped a hay rope around the flywheel and pulled the engine out with a team of horses. They move real easy this way, as the gearing gives you a lot of leverage. My first job was to clean the flues. Dad backed our old buckboard in front of the engine so I would have a place to stand. I couldn't reach the top flues, but the old buckboard did the trick. Then there was brass to polish and general cleaning. We always had a pail of Black Beauty axle grease, which worked wonders on the gearing. Then the oil man arrived with a barrel of steam cylinder oil, which had a wonderful smell to it.

The final job was to clean the grain bins of what was left of last year's grain. We did not have overhead bins or elevators; all we had was a No. 12 or No. 14 scoop shovel, which wasn't too bad to use once you get the hang of it. We hauled the grain to the elevator in a triple-box wagon. We were lucky as we had a spring seat. Those old wooden wheel wagons didn't absorb very much shock.

It was late September before we could thresh, the time of year when you could hear the whooping crane down in the swamp or the loon calling his mate in the evening. You could also see a few geese in their perfect formation taking their time heading south.

It's Saturday, 5:30 a.m., and everybody is up and going. The first thing I hear is my orders: "We need more wood for the cookstove, then better get a couple pails of fresh water, then you might dig a few more potatoes." I am hurrying because I wanted to get to where the action is: the thresher. My next chore is to hitch old Nellie to the buggy, find a couple stone jugs, wrap them with burlap and wet them down to keep them cool. My job is to haul drinking water to the help.

Soon old Jake Cain came down the dirt road with his rake wagon pulled by his team of beautiful Belgians. You could smell the freshly oiled harness, see all of the fittings highly polished, and hear those wooden wheels moving back and forth on the skeins. Next came Rufe McNickles in his old Dodge Touring car with four bundle pitchers.

By 7 a.m., I hear a little toot on the engine, and with a little puff of smoke, the old 20hp Advance came to life. The Advance was pulling a 40in Port Huron separator. I heard the belt slap a couple of times and then I heard Dad say, "Block her." By this time, the separator was up to speed. The separator man yelled, "Throw 'em in boys, head first." Then two more men climbed on to the rack—spike pitchers. As the bundle haulers started in, a prairie chicken woke up here and there across the fields. We had a little over 100 acres of small grain that year and the grain was dry and in great shape.

The old 20hp sidemounted Advance engine was running great. Dad had the buckboard backed up to the engine. The buckboard was full of coal, which was broken down to fist size or smaller before it was put in the firebox. The small size of the coal made for faster heat. This engine was not hard on water and fired easy—it was one heck of an engine! I knew every bolt and nut on that engine and what they were used for.

One thing you didn't hear in those days was an engine popping off. There were a lot of young, spirited horses and you didn't need a lot of confusion with runaway teams. Not only that, but popping an engine was a waste of water and fuel. Engines were popped before the threshing day started. An engineer who couldn't control his boiler pressure was dubbed a poor engineer. Water was pumped into the tank by hand, so you didn't waste too much. Dad used to admonish me to "know where the water is in your boiler—the fire can go out, but don't run out of water."

It wasn't long until the noon whistle blew announcing dinnertime. Horses were tied to the feed box on the back of the racks to be fed and watered, then everyone headed for the yard. A tub of soft water sat on a bench with two or three bars of soap at the ready. An old mirror hung on a tree nearby; linen towels hung on the clothesline.

Dinner was a great time with roast beef, mashed potatoes, gravy, sweet corn on the cob, homemade bread, strawberry jam, and other things making it almost a Thanksgiving feast.

Then came the goodies: apple pie, cherry pie, cakes, and cookies. You ate until you almost burst.

After lunch, you gathered in the yard for a little idle chatter. You could look on the horizon in any direction and see a column of idle smoke riding into the sky from different rigs. Dad had gone to the engine earlier to check up on things; a little toot on the whistle and things were humming again.

It wasn't long until evening was there. Another threshing day was over, everything sat quiet. Chaff was scattered all over the place.

There were all makes of engines in those days and they were all good. Every engineer had his choice, a natural thing. But it wasn't long until tractors started to cut in on the steam engine. At the time of World War II, a lot of top-notch engines fell to the hands of the torch. We threshed until 1948, and the last couple of years we used a W40 International pulling a 28in Red River Special. This was a fine rig, but it didn't have the character of the steam rig.

In the late thirties, the combine arrived. They were of the smaller types—5-9ft was average. By then, everybody wanted to do their own grain and not have to go through threshing rings. We lost out on those fabulous dinners and the closeness among the neighbors. As for the binders, a lot of real good ones fell to the torch to make windrowers.

These days, we have been reliving the old times at the great steam threshing shows. We bought our 18-50 Case in 1985. We have 28in and 32in Case separators but usually use the 32in. We thresh here at home every year. Mom cooks up a lot of goodies and the neighbors also bring in cakes, pies, and more so we can have a regular picnic under the trees. The kids really enjoy it, climbing on Grandad's engine and tooting the whistle.

My good friend Don Vogeler, an old boiler man, has been around when I needed help with something. He is good with an engine. My other good friend Albert Brown, who has his own machine shop, helps when I need something made. He is a perfectionist—true quality work!

My daughter, Judy, and my two sons, Jim and John, and their families took to steam like ducks to water. Maybe they will keep it going for years to come. Don't forget the steam oil!

J.I. CASE THRESHING MACHINE CO.,
RACINE. WIS. U.S.A.

The Threshing Machine Comes of Age

. . . here be threshing instruments . . .
—2 Samuel 24:22

By the time of the American Civil War, the threshing machine was a well-developed tool of farm production. It was made mainly of wood, and its size was limited by the requirements of portability and by the number of horses needed to turn it. But it was, within the above limitations, a mature technology.

Three elements were still needed to bring the concept to final fruition: ancillary equipment, such as feeders and stackers; the steam engine for power; and brilliant industrial pioneers, such as J. I. Case, the Masseys, McCormick, and Deering, to build and distribute these giant machines at a reasonable price.

Like subsequent wars, the Civil War did much to advance technology and industrialization. It also did much to diversify farming, and hence, an increased demand for a variety of farm machinery, which aided in the establishment of large equipment manufacturing plants. For example, increased demand by the Army for beef and pork caused many farmers to shift from wheat to coarser feed grains.

The Civil War also greatly accelerated the development of the railroad as a means of transporting troops and equipment, but also allowed the shipment of large pieces of farm machinery at a reasonable cost.

Previous page
This pictorial logo shows the J. I. Case factory in Racine, Wisconsin. It graces an 1888 wooden Case thresher.

Threshing scene, Manitoba, Canada, in the late twenties.

This miraculously well-preserved 1888 wooden Case threshing machine is now owned by the Stephenson County, Illinois, Antique Engine Club, who purchased it from a club member, Robert Lamb. It was originally purchased by A. and D. Hoesley, farmers near New Glarus, Wisconsin. The Hoesleys, and subsequent owners, used it for seventy-five years in their annual threshings. The machine is hand-fed and has no bundle cutter and no blower, but does have the bagger attachment, as shown.

Finally, the war brought increased competition for the remaining farm laborers—and hence, higher pay. This, in turn, made the cash layout for such equipment as automatic binders and threshing machines more justifiable.

Thus, the last half of the nineteenth century saw great changes in world agriculture, but the effects were mostly felt in the United States and Canada, which would from then on assume responsibility for feeding themselves and much of the rest of the world.

These effects were felt in the Grain Belt more dramatically than perhaps anywhere else—and not only on the farms, because the large cities of the Great Plains became the industrial centers of farm machinery production. The demands of the cities for workers only aggravated the farm labor shortage. On the farms, it was a period of relatively good weather and stable market demands. In short, it was a time of prosperity for those who could make the switch to mechanized farming and could keep up with the labor demands.

Feeders and Stackers

Before 1880, two members of the threshing crew had to stand at the feeding table of the threshing machine. One was the band cutter and one was the feeder. Next to the separator man, or boss, the feeder was the most important man on the crew. Properly feeding the big machine took skill and experience.

The band cutter severed the bundle twine or wires and passed the bundles to the feeder, who spread them out and fed them headfirst into the cylinder hopper. His job was to regulate the amount of straw and grain passing through the cylinder at any one time to prevent overloading and choking. This could plug up the machine, which would mean a shutdown, or at least, cause inefficient threshing. It was also important for the grain to be spread out over the entire width of the cylinder to use most of the machine's capacity. Good feeding was essential for a fast and clean job of threshing.

In the last quarter of the nineteenth century, the self-feeding attachment came into use. This welcome device eliminated the highly skilled, tedious, and dirty job of hand feeding. The self-feeder consisted of a slatted conveyor called the bundle carrier, a band cutter,

The input drive gear, or crown wheel, for the 1888 Case thresher. The input shaft, from the left, is driven by a horse-powered treadmill. Behind the shaft is a small bevel gear on the cylinder shaft, which mates with the input gear. Above the mesh is a screw-down grease cup.

and a cylinder feeding/regulating apparatus.

Two men were usually still required for feeding, but now they stood on the bundle wagon and simply pitched the bundles onto the conveyor, grain-end

There is no automatic band cutter or self feeder on this 1888 wooden Case threshing machine. There is also no blower, so dust from the grain can get into the bearings and cause a fire. Grain was pushed head-first into the teeth of the rotating cylinder visible at the end of the chute.

33

Straw and chaff are expelled from the back of this 1888 Case thresher and onto a straw elevator. Men with forks then had to move the straw away from where the elevator dropped it.

first, with long-handled forks. The conveyor carried the bundles under the row of reciprocating knives, placed just before the cylinder, which chopped the twine bands into pieces too small to clog the machine. Then, the regulating mechanism caused the bottom part of the bundle to be held back while the top straws were peeled off and fed into the

The straw end of the 1888 wooden Case thresher. Note the cat-whiskers which keep the straw from going back and forth with the action of the agitator. This causes the straw to migrate through the machine and out onto the straw elevator to the right.

Previous page
The tailings elevator of the 1888 Case thresher carried unthreshed heads and other material too large to go through the sieve, but too small to be carried out with the straw, back to the cylinder for reprocessing.

Without a stacker, straw piles up in one spot and must be moved away by hand. This pile, on the end of the 1888 Case machine, is just about as high as it can go.

This is the clutch mechanism, which goes between the horse-powered treadmill and the threshing machine. It is staked down into the sod to keep it from moving.

Next page
Once the horses are in motion, the clutch (belt tightener) is engaged, starting the thresher. This scene from the 22nd Annual Old-fashioned Threshing Show at Freeport, Illinois, shows how labor-intensive threshing was in the nineteenth century.

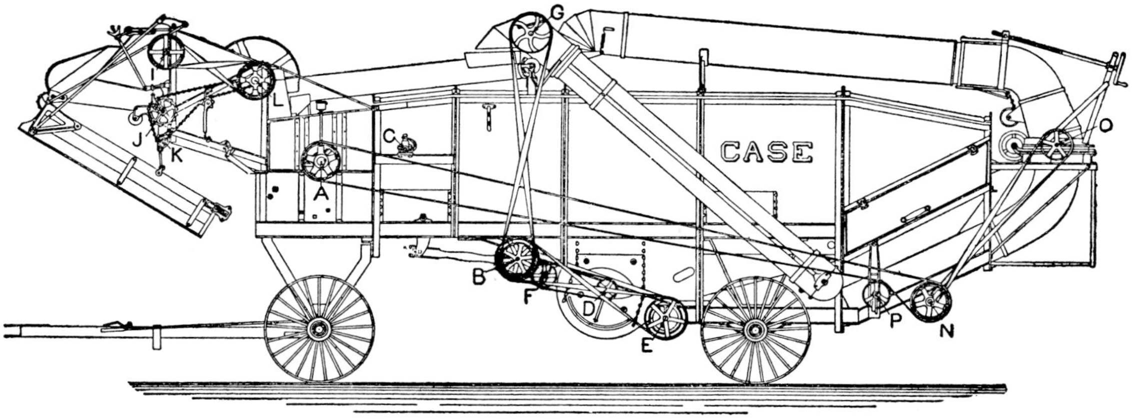

FIG. 45. RIGHT SIDE OF BELT SEPARATOR WITH FEEDER AND WIND STACKER.

Number	Shaft.	Diameter.	Face.	Bore.	Name.
501T	A	8¼	8	1⅝	Main drive pulley, 36 and 42″.
5004T	A	9¼	9	1⅝	Main drive pulley, 46″.
5294T	A	13½	9	2 7/16	Main drive pulley, 50″ and up.
A301H	A	12	5¼	2 7/16	Pulley drives wind stacker, 50, 54 and 58″.
A296H	A	13⅜	5¼	2 7/16	Pulley drives wind stacker, 62 and 66″.
B130H	A	9	5¼	1⅝	Pulley drives wind stacker, 36, 42 and 46″.
324H	P	9	5⅞	1	Tightener pulley.
A165H	N	12¼	5¼	1½	Pulley on wind stacker shaft.
331H	N	3	2¼	1½	Pulley drives oscillating device.
864T	O	9½	2½	15/16	Pulley on oscillating device shaft.

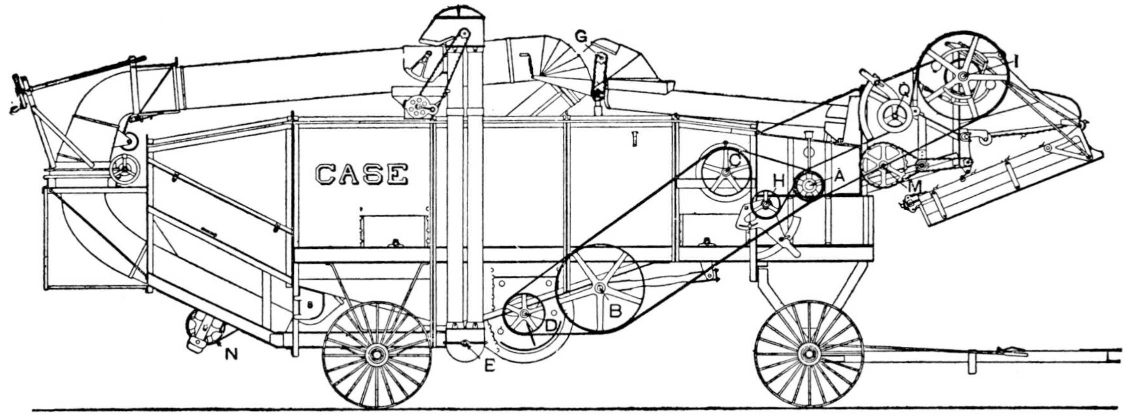

FIG. 46. LEFT SIDE OF SEPARATOR WITH FEEDER, WEIGHER AND WIND STACKER.

Number	Shaft	Diameter	Face	Bore	Name
1348T	A	5¾	4½	1⅝	Pulley drives crank, beater and fan, 46″ and under.
5365T	A	8½	6¼	2 7/16	Pulley drives crank, beater and fan, 50″ and up.
A971T	B	28	4¼	1⅜	Pulley on crank shaft, 46″ and under.
A1078T	B	28	6¼	1⅜	Pulley on crank shaft, 50″ and up.
A1255T	C	15¾	4½	1 3/16	Pulley on beater shaft, 46″ and under.
A1254T	C	15¾	6¼	1 3/16	Pulley on beater shaft, 50″ and up.
5433T	D	13⅛	4¼	1 3/16	Pulley on fan shaft.
1682T	H	9	6¼	1⅜	Tightener pulley, 50″ and up.
1684T	H	9	4¼	1⅜	Tightener pulley, 46″ and under.
5093T	A	6¾	4¼	1⅝	Pulley drives feeder, 46″ and under.
5295T	A	9½	4¼	2 3/16	Pulley drives feeder, 50″ and up.
5224T	I	28	4¼	1⅜	Pulley on feeder crank.
5542T	Q	7⅝	4¼	1⅜	Tightener.
61FS		6 teeth, No. 32 chain			Sprocket drives retarder.
20FS	M	32 teeth, No. 32 chain			Sprocket on retarder shaft.
5542T	Q	7½	4¼	1⅜	Tightener pulley all feeders.

cylinder in much the same way as hand feeding was done. If the cylinder became overloaded, a governor would cause all feeding to stop until the cylinder began to clear. When choking did occur, it was referred to as slugging, a term still used in the air-conditioning trade to indicate a liquid lock in the compressor.

The self-stacker made its debut somewhat earlier than the feeder. Early threshing machines simply dumped the straw on the ground behind the machine, where pitchers forked it either on a wagon for hauling or away from the machine so that the operation could continue.

Straw was a valuable commodity around the farm, and had a number of uses, such as animal bedding, plant covering, and in many cases, fuel for the steam engine. A large stack of straw was also a status symbol, of sorts, in the farming community: a sign of prosperity.

Straw was left outside, tightly wrapped together to shed moisture, and the piling was somewhat of an art, whether done by hand or machine. With the machines introduced in about 1870, piles could rise as high as 30ft. Even with machine stacking, men were needed to work the piles into the proper proportion of diameter and height. This meant estimating, at the start, the proper diameter of the pile and then gradually drawing in the sides as the pile grew higher, and finally, topping it out with the last bit of straw from the machine.

The first type of stacker to arrive on the scene, eliminating the dirtiest of all the threshing jobs, was simply a

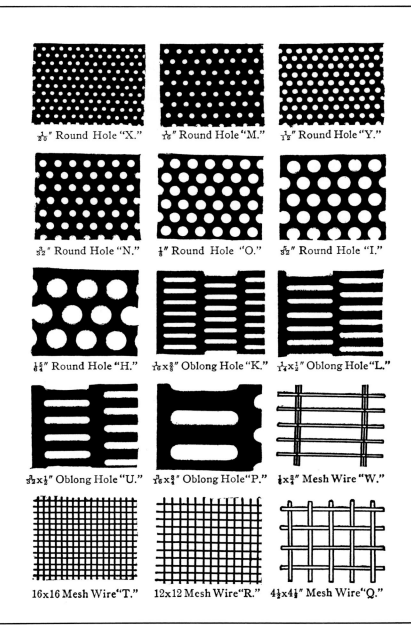

$\frac{1}{20}$" Round Hole "X." $\frac{1}{8}$" Round Hole "M." $\frac{1}{12}$" Round Hole "Y."

$\frac{3}{32}$" Round Hole "N." $\frac{1}{8}$" Round Hole "O." $\frac{5}{32}$" Round Hole "I."

$\frac{15}{64}$" Round Hole "H." $\frac{1}{16}$x$\frac{3}{8}$" Oblong Hole "K." $\frac{1}{14}$x$\frac{1}{2}$" Oblong Hole "L."

$\frac{3}{32}$x$\frac{1}{2}$" Oblong Hole "U." $\frac{3}{16}$x$\frac{3}{4}$" Oblong Hole "P." $\frac{1}{4}$x$\frac{3}{4}$" Mesh Wire "W."

16x16 Mesh Wire "T." 12x12 Mesh Wire "R." 4$\frac{1}{2}$x4$\frac{1}{2}$" Mesh Wire "Q."

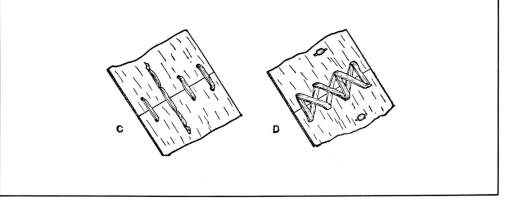

C   D

Lacing for 4in thresher belt.

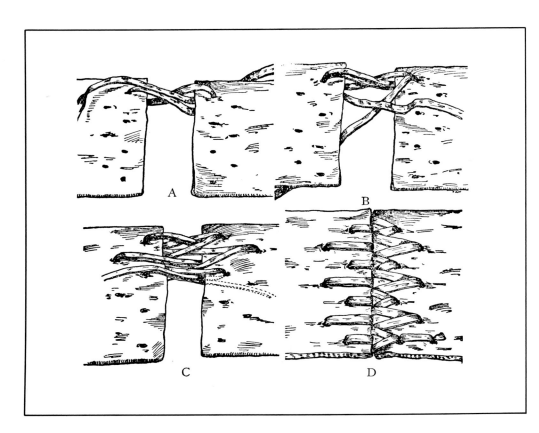

A   B

C   D

conveyor of slats and chain attached to the end of the machine and driven by an additional flat belt. The conveyor, or elevator, as it was then called, alleviated the problem of what to do with the straw, but did not eliminate it altogether. If threshing continued until the straw piled up to the end of the conveyor, pitching had to begin or the machine had to be moved forward.

During the 1880s, swing-stackers began replacing the stationary conveyor. These could be moved from side to side to make semi-circular piles of straw, some with arcs of almost 180 degrees. The earliest of the swing-stackers were not supported by the threshing machine itself, but were on a separate running gear, though still driven by a belt from the machine. Later swing-stackers were attached to the machine, and were also moved from side to side automatically by power from the machine.

To remain attached during transport, the stacker conveyors came in two sections which folded upon themselves on top of the machine. Some sections

Sectional view of a J. I. Case feeder.

Sectional view of the head of a J. I. Case weigher.

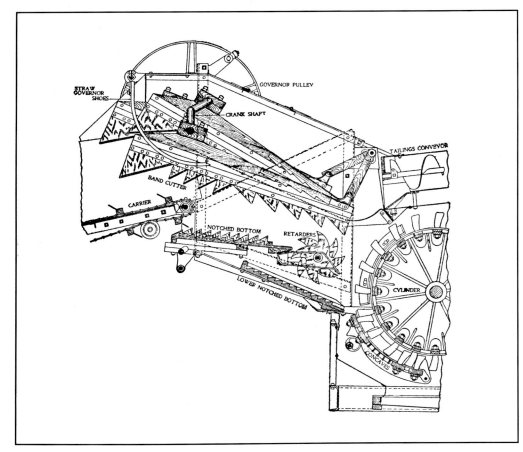

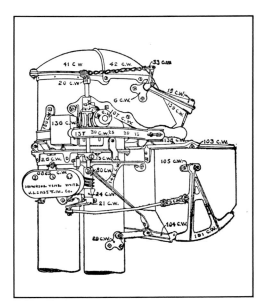

were as long as 20ft, producing a total conveyor length of 40ft.

At almost the same time that the swing-stacker was introduced, an Indianapolis, Indiana, inventor named James Buchanan patented a device he called the wind stacker. It consisted of a centrifugal blower and a telescoping tube. The blower drew straw and chaff from the rear of the machine and carried it on the discharge airflow, out the tube. The tube had an elbow on the end which directed the straw down into a pile, while the chaff and dust were blasted into the air. Wind stackers could be oscillated and their angles adjusted to make several straw stacks or a continuous semi-circular stack.

Although there were problems with the wind stacker, it soon almost displaced the swinging conveyor type. The main problem was that farmers suspected that the wind stacker sucked out the grain with the straw. While some was carried away, the wind stacker was at least as efficient as any other type. Second, wind stackers cost

A threshing rig folded up and ready to move.

more than even the most elaborate conveyor stackers. Third, they consumed considerable horsepower and, until the advent of the steam engine, they were not practical. Fourth, they were noisy, adding to the already noisy operation of the cylinder. Finally, prevailing winds could direct the blowing straw and chaff back onto the threshing crew. Thus, wind direction now became another factor in setting up a thresher; as often happened, a change in wind direction meant resetting the machine.

With perfection of feeders and stackers, the threshing machine was complete and, for the most part, in its final form. What was now needed were the source of adequate power to run them (steam) and entrepreneurs to build and distribute them in reliable and affordable form.

The Arrival of Steam Power

When water is converted to steam at 212deg. Fahrenheit (sea level standard pressure), it expands 1,600 times. Confining the vapor causes a rapid and dramatic pressure increase inside of the confining vessel. Expanded pressure also raises the boiling temperature, which further increases the energy available from the steam. As is true throughout the history of engines, from the steam engine to modern gas turbines, progress is predicated upon metallurgy. Because of

the strength of the iron and the methods available to make seams, early engines were limited to fewer than 100psi pressure.

Metallurgy also limited the means of extracting the power once generated in the form of steam. The strength of materials dictated the size and weight of pistons, connecting rods, and gears. Reciprocating weight had to be balanced, and as rotating and reciprocating weight increased, allowable operating speed decreased. Since horsepower is a rate of doing work, reducing the speed worked against the desired end result.

Before the middle of the nineteenth century, steam engines were so large and heavy (because the iron in the boiler was so thick and because of conservative stresses in rotating and reciprocating parts) that portability was not even considered, except for railroads. By the 1870s, the Bessemer steelmaking process made relatively lightweight, but powerful, steam engines a reality.

All steam engines, regardless of the manufacturer, had common elements: smokestack, boiler, engine (cylinders, pistons, and valves), governor, flywheel, and firebox. Heat and smoke from the firebox passed through flues, or tubes, in the boiler on their way to the smokestack. Water surrounding the flues would soon be heated to the boiling temperature, and pressure would be raised to as much as 200psi (in later designs). The pressurized steam then was admitted into the cylinder through valves—and the engine was in business. Upon this theme there were, however, many variations.

First, there could be a frame to which the boiler and other parts were attached, or the boiler could be used as the frame. Then there was the matter of a direct, or return-flue, boiler. With the direct boiler, the stack was mounted on the end opposite the firebox, and the heat made just one pass through the water. As its name implies, two passes were made by the heat in the return-flue type, and the stack was on the same end as the firebox. Then there could be two-cylinder versus one-cylinder engines, and there could be single-acting or double-acting pistons.

Early farm steam engines were just that: portable power plants. It wasn't until the 1880s or late 1870s that self-propelled steam engines came into being. Even then, the first of these required horses to be hitched to the front axle for steering. The driver sometimes rode on the engine and held the reins, or walked along the side. At least now, the thresher could move his whole outfit at once: water tender, fuel trailer, and threshing machine.

In the early 1880s, self-steering was added, and steam engines became "traction engines," with many more ways to earn their keep around the farm. From then until 1915, their numbers and their power grew dramatically. In 1890, some 3,000 engines were produced in the United States. By 1900, that number had risen to 5,000, and by 1915, it had doubled.

Early engines were 8-10hp; by 1910, this grew to an average of 40hp. Some of the largest, destined for plowing the western plains, produced as much as 120hp and weighed more than 50,000lb.

A 40hp steam engine was ideal for handling a 32in separator with a wind stacker. For a day's work, about two cords of wood and about 500 gallons of water were needed. Rates of production varied a great deal, depending on conditions, the size of the crew, and whether resetting was required, but basically, about ten bushels of wheat per horsepower-hour was a rule of thumb. A 1903 issue of *Implement Trade Journal* lists a record 4,071 bushels of wheat threshed in a single day by a single crew with a single rig. The separator was an Avery 42x70, driven by an Avery 30hp engine. Work began at sunrise and continued until a half-hour after sunset. One move was required during the day, and there was a 45 minute delay caused by a 5lb ball of twine falling into the maw of the separator.

Such a production record serves to dramatically indicate the magnitude of the change in agriculture in the last half of the nineteenth century. The steel plow, the self-binding harvester, the threshing machine, and the steam engine raised the amount of grain one man could plant and harvest in a year from fewer than ten acres to more than three hundred. In addition, the mechanized farmer had time for other things, as well.

Steam power was not, however, a panacea. A steam engine required the complete attention of the engineer. Low water level in the boiler was always an alarming discovery. If water could not be replenished instantly, the fire had to be pulled from the firebox. In some cases, quickly elevating the front of the engine kept the remaining water over the firebox to prevent cracking of the "crown" or flues. Sometimes, as a result of cracks, rust, or weak metal, explosions could occur, with disastrous results. In 1914, records indicate a boiler explosion rate of two per day. In about one-third of these, the operator was killed.

Another problem with steam power was inadequate bridge strength. Wooden bridges were designed for horse-pulled loads, but a 12ton traction engine was another story. Originally, municipalities had little sympathy for the thresher crews, passing laws that made them liable for bridge damage.

In a world dominated by horses, the appearance of the steam engine caused a rash of highway accidents. Even experienced horsemen found their teams difficult to control when a traction engine approached. Communities quickly passed laws regulating the use of public roads and seriously restricting the operation of a self-propelled conveyance. In some cases, the engineer was required to hitch horses to the front of the machine, to allay the fears of approaching horses. Other laws forbade blowing the whistle or required a man to walk fifty yards ahead to warn approaching drivers. The now-familiar signs forbidding vehicles with cleats or lugs to use highways made their debut as a result of the traction engine.

Finally, the steam engine was a constant source of fire danger. One of the reasons for the long belt to the thresher was to reduce the risk of a spark from the stack reaching the straw pile. Another danger was simply setting afire the stubble around the engine.

By the advent of World War I, gasoline and kerosene tractors were rapidly replacing steam. The Fordson was introduced in 1917, giving internal-combustion power to even the smallest farmer. In 1924, International Harvester introduced the first Farmall row crop tractor—and the age of steam was over. J. I. Case was the largest producer of steam engines, followed closely by Huber. Manufacturers succumbed to Madison Avenue techniques in selecting names that suggested speed and power, such as the Robinson "Conqueror," the Port Huron "Rusher," the Geiser "Peerless," the Harrison "Jumbo," the Advance "Incomparable," the Monitor "Champion," and the Minneapolis "Little Giant." Case was, however, the only major steam engine maker to successfully make the switch to internal combustion.

Heroes of the Realm: J. I. Case

In the middle part of the nineteenth century, when transportation, communication, power for

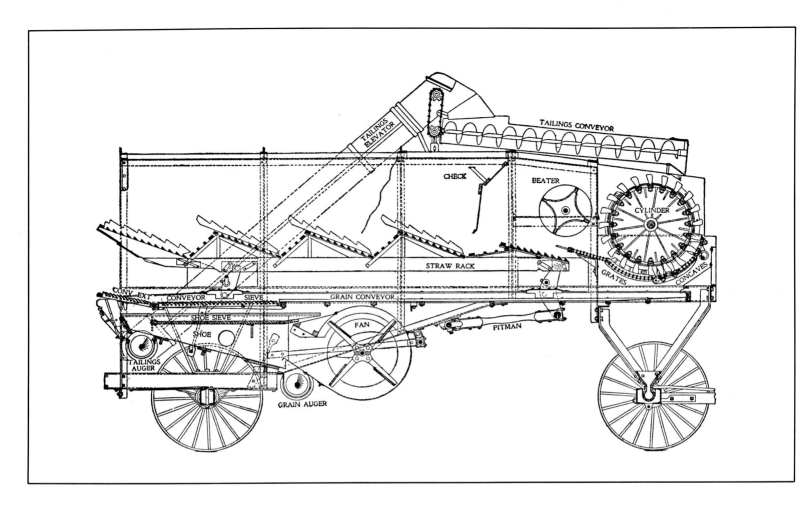

Sectional view of a J. I. Case separator.

manufacturing, and finance were nothing at all like we enjoy today, there was a revolution in agricultural mechanization. It was during this time that three giants arose in the land: the J. I. Case Company, Massey Harris Company, Ltd., and the International Harvester Company. The founders of these companies had a rare combination of inventive genius, perseverance, and business sense. Without their stories, the picture of the threshing machine would be only a sketch.

Jerome Increase Case was born in Oswego, New York, on December 11, 1819. He was the son of Caleb Case, a farmer, and Deborah Jackson Case, of the family that produced President Andrew Jackson.

Caleb Case bought one of the first groundhog threshing machines when Jerome was just a lad. Naturally, young

Jerome assisted his father with its operation. The long hours gave him ample time to consider its limitations. It also became apparent to Jerome that the future of grain harvesting was not in the lake area of New York, but in the Upper Mississippi River Valley and in the Great Plains of the Midwest.

Stories trickling back told of homesteaders who had the potential of raising vast acres of wheat but virtually no farm labor, except for the family. Case, then twenty-two years old, sensed his opportunity. On credit, he bought six Pitts groundhog threshers and horse-powered treadmills and started west by rail for a frontier town called Chicago.

During the harvest of 1842, Case sold five of the six groundhogs, keeping one for custom threshing. He finally settled in the town of Rochester, in the territory of Wisconsin, not far from the town of Racine.

During the winter of 1842-1843, Case built himself a threshing machine

designed along the groundhog line, but with improvements. Case was pleased with the performance of his machine during the harvest of 1843. With that, Case rented a shop in Racine to manufacture threshers for the next season.

Up until this point, threshing machines did only that: they threshed the heads from the stalks and then deposited the whole works on the ground below the machine. Case saw the benefit of combining the fanning mill directly into the thresher. He sought out Richard Ela, a fanning mill maker from New Hampshire, and with his help, Case incorporated a fan into the design of his machine, which he had ready for the harvest of 1844, a machine which would both thresh and separate, depositing the straw in one location and cleaned grain in another.

To say that the Case separating thresher was a success would be an understatement; by 1847, a new plant had been constructed, complete with its own steam power plant and its own foundry. Case, not yet thirty years old, had become Racine's largest employer.

Next, Case acquired patent rights for a vibrator apparatus designed as an add-on to the groundhog thresher, and built it into his machine. These were produced, with periodic improvements, for about fifteen years, along with horse-powered treadmills of Case's design. In 1869, the Case Eclipse thresher was introduced. This was an apron-less machine which pioneered the use of straw racks. Also in 1869, the first Case steam engine was belted to a threshing machine. In 1892, the year after J. I. Case died, the first internal combustion traction engine rolled out for testing.

The J. I. Case Company had become a corporation in 1880, with J. I. Case as president. With able officers in place, the company continued to prosper even after the death of its founder. It went on to become a full-line producer of agricultural and industrial machinery.

Massey-Harris Threshers

Daniel Massey had his first shop in operation for two years when J. I. Case opened his. It is doubtful that Massey thought of himself as an industrialist, however, since the main reason for the shop was the repair of his own farm machinery. By 1840, D. Massey was already forty-one years old, and a successful Canadian farmer with more than 200 acres under cultivation.

When Daniel was an infant, his father (also named Daniel) and his mother, Rebecca, had migrated from their home in New York State across Lake Ontario. The reasons for their migration are not known for sure, but the lure of inexpensive land on the Lake Ontario Plain was probably among them.

Daniel was only thirteen years old when his father left him in charge of the farm and went into the militia for the War of 1812. During his father's absence, young Daniel hired men to plant and harvest, and upon his return, he found that the lad had managed the farm with an ability far beyond his years.

Soon after his nineteenth birthday, Massey left his father's farm and struck out on his own on rented land a few miles away. Although the land was

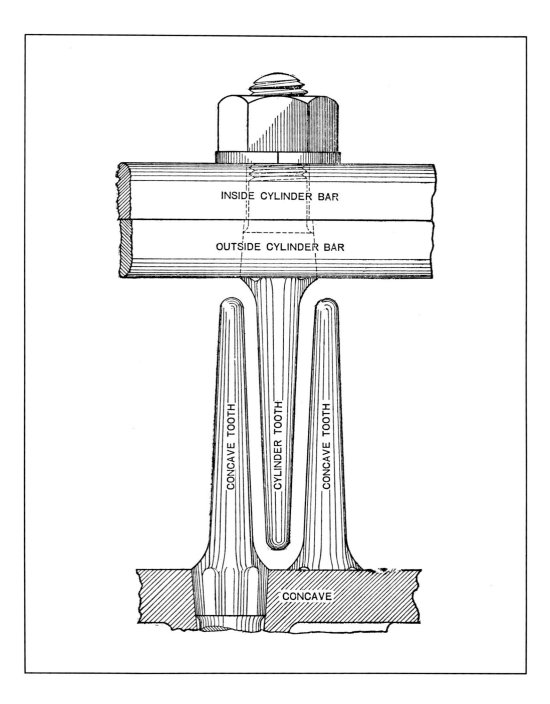

INSIDE CYLINDER BAR

OUTSIDE CYLINDER BAR

CONCAVE TOOTH   CYLINDER TOOTH   CONCAVE TOOTH

CONCAVE

Cut showing the space between teeth.

Next page
In 1921, J. I. Case's threshers reigned supreme among farmers.

forested, Massey began clearing it and found that he had a ready market for the pine logs. He also had no difficulty in hiring the help he needed to clear the land, as this was a period of great immigration. By the time he was twenty-one, Massey owned 200 acres, free and clear.

Simultaneous lumbering and farming occupied Massey's next twelve years. He would buy a forested tract of land, clear it, and then farm it until it could be sold as farmland. At times, he employed as many as 100 men. By 1829, much of the Lake Ontario Plain had been cleared, and wheat farming was increasingly becoming the main activity.

Are You Canvassing Thresher Prospects?

THRESHERMEN and farmers are now checking up on grain acreage for the year and analyzing the opportunities for new threshing rigs. Are you doing the same? If not, we suggest that you check up the threshermen and farmers in your vicinity who need new machines.

Farmers this year are going to be more insistent than ever about a real job of threshing.

They will demand:

Clean threshing; thorough separation; perfect cleaning; unequalled saving.

With a Case Thresher:

They can thresh grain from the heads *clean*, by the use of the scientifically designed Case cylinder.

They get *thorough separation* from the violent agitation of the Case balanced straw Rack.

They secure *perfect cleaning* through the Case adjustable sieves, end shake shoe and full width, underblast fan.

They are finally assured of *unequalled saving of grain* and protected against possible losses that might result from faulty thresher adjustment, by the Case Grain-Saving Wind Stacker.

Send us the names of thresher prospects in your vicinity so that we can co-operate with you in developing their interest in Case Threshing Machines. This will result in sales that will mean more profits to you.

J. I. Case Threshing Machine Company

Dept. D-213   Racine,   Wisconsin

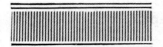

CASE

TRADE MARKS REG. U.S. PAT OFF.   AND IN FOREIGN COUNTRIES.

THRESHING MACHINES

This International Harvester thresher, from around 1950, represents the ultimate in thresher design. These models were so reliable that ads boasted that a full-time separator man was not required.

In 1830, Massey returned from a trip to the United States with a Pope thresher, which he set up in his barn. Although crude and inefficient, it marked a turning point in Massey's life; his interest in labor-saving farm machinery had been sparked.

International Harvester logo on a late-model thresher. International Harvester, originally using the brand name McCormick-Deering, brought out its line of all-steel machines in 1925, and production continued through 1956; one of the last companies to produce threshers.

McCormick-Deering threshers were noted for their light-running characteristics because of the use of ball anti-friction bearings.

The next fifteen years also saw great changes in Canadian economics and agriculture. Red Fife wheat, the parent of all Canadian hard wheats, was introduced, and with it, a boom in wheat growing. It was also a time of emigration, because of Canadian prosperity and of hardships in Europe. But the prosperity ended when British free-trade policies eliminated Canada's advantage in the sale of flour. This and other ill-advised protectionist trade policies, coupled with a poor harvest of 1847, abruptly ended the good times.

The economic downturn forced the closing of a small foundry and machine

shop in Bond Head, Ontario, owned by R. F. Vaughan, a friend of Daniel Massey. Soon, Vaughan and Massey formed a partnership for the manufacture of farm machinery. Massey turned his farm over to his twenty-one-year-old son, Hart. By the second year of operation, Massey had bought out his partner, and had bought new property in nearby Newcastle for expansion.

The Newcastle Foundry and Machine Manufactory thrived by making small implements, mostly through acquired American patents, and a good harvest in 1850 brought in more business than the little company could handle. The now fifty-two-year-old Massey brought his son, Hart, into the business. While the younger Massey was not the inventor that his father was, he had an instinctive sense of recognizing a useful

invention. By 1852, Hart had become full partner and general manager, and Daniel took a less-active role. Then, in 1855, Daniel retired and Hart became sole proprietor. At age fifty-eight, Daniel Massey died.

An advertisement in *The Newcastle Recorder* in 1857 listed 4, 6, and 8hp "thrashing" machines among a wide variety of products by Hart Massey's Newcastle Manufactory.

Alanson Harris opened his implement business in 1857, and soon became one of Hart Massey's strongest competitors. Born in 1816, the son of a circuit-riding minister preaching the Baptist faith to the Canadians north of Lake Ontario, Alanson also had responsibility thrust upon him at an early age. While his father was off riding his circuit, duties of the family farm fell to nine-year-old Alanson and

This late-model International Harvester/ McCormick-Deering thresher used the company's own brand of feeder.

local parishioners. The Reverend Harris disdained the hard labor of farming, and was always scheming to find a way to mechanize the effort; he had made some progress toward the perfection of a horse-pulled rotary hay rake. At age thirteen, Alanson went to work in a local sawmill to supplement the family income.

Harris worked at the mill for more than ten years, eventually marrying into money and buying a mill of his own, which he operated for another fifteen years. Harris recognized the changes coming in economics and agriculture; because of these and because the pine forests of the district

were all but gone, he sold the mill in 1856 and opened an implement company in Beamsville, Ontario. Harris had apparently inherited his father's mechanical inquisitiveness.

Duplicating the Massey story, Harris took his son, John, into the business in 1863. The business prospered and expanded, mostly through the use of others' patents. There was intense competition between Hart Massey and Alanson Harris to recognize which inventions to acquire, and to do so before the other. The two struggled for recognition in the British Empire and world implement markets, but were generally thwarted by politics at trade fairs and in the press. Finally in 1891, the two sons, Hart and John, agreed to merge their firms to become one of the world's largest implement manufacturers: Massey-Harris.

The new Canadian implement giant undertook further growth toward becoming a full-line company by acquiring forty percent interest in Verity Plow Company of Exeter, Ontario, and L. D. Sawyer Company of Hamilton, Ontario. Sawyer, now Sawyer-Massey Company, Ltd., was a manufacturer of threshing machines and steam tractors. After the turn of the century, the Geo. White and Sons Company, Ltd., a producer of several sizes of threshers, of London, Ontario, was also acquired. With the acquisition of White, the interest in Sawyer was sold in 1910.

International Harvester Threshers

Cyrus McCormick was born to Robert and Mary Ann on February 15, 1809. His father was by then a fairly wealthy

49

Elwin Swegle of Ashton, Illinois, demonstrates a 1940 McCormick-Deering PTO binder at the 1991 Franklin Grove, Illinois, thresheree. Many wagon-loads of bundled grain are required each year for thresherees. This means that each club must designate some land to grow wheat, oats, or both, do the planting according to the thresheree schedule, and then get the grain cut, bundled, and hauled to the site—a series of tasks that show the dedication of those attempting to preserve this glimpse of history for others to enjoy.

Virginia farmer, with more than 500 acres of land. His estate had its own grist mill, sawmill, and blacksmith shop. Robert tinkered with the invention of a mechanical reaper as early as 1809, but success was to wait for his son, Cyrus Hall McCormick.

By 1847, the McCormick Harvesting Machine Company had already been in business for more than seven years, and was bursting at the seams. Like J. I. Case, Cyrus recognized that the market for grain harvesting equipment was farther west. On August 30, 1847, McCormick entered into a partnership with C. M. Gray of Chicago. While McCormick was away from Chicago, Gray sold half of his half-interest in the new company to Messrs. Ogden and Jones. Needless to say, McCormick was upset over the arrangement and took Gray to court. While the matter was awaiting decision, Gray sold the remaining portion of his interest to Ogden. Thus, in 1848, the business was renamed McCormick, Ogden and Company, with Jones still a junior partner. By September of the next year, Ogden and Jones sold their interests to McCormick for $65,000.

To help him run his burgeoning business, Cyrus invited his brothers, Leander and William, to come to Chicago. Things went well until William died in 1865, and acrimony arose over the distribution of his estate. Cyrus and Leander did not get along well from then on. In 1879, the partnership was changed into a corporation, with Cyrus holding three-fourths of the stock and Leander, the balance.

Cyrus H. McCormick died in 1884, after witnessing the great revolution in mechanized agriculture, after acquiring great wealth, and after seeing his reaper company grow to the largest of its kind. His widow and son, Cyrus Jr., bought out Leander's interest in 1890. By this time, however, the company's preeminence in the field was being seriously challenged, because McCormick had been too slow in picking up promising new invention rights—the slowness due in the most

The Aultman Company, not to be confused with Aultman-Taylor of Mansfield, Ohio, shows its wares in this 1901 ad. Note the American uses a geared wind stacker.

part to the bickering between the brothers.

William Deering was one of those to capitalize on McCormick's slowness. McCormick had been in the reaper business for about forty years when Deering, then forty-four years old, bought into the rights to the Marsh harvester.

Before entering the implement business, William Deering had made a substantial fortune in the wholesale dry goods business in Maine. In 1870, he made his way to Chicago to invest in some land, but happened to call on an acquaintance named Elijah Gammon, a retired Methodist preacher, who had become a partner in the firm that was attempting to manufacture the Marsh harvester. Gammon persuaded Deering to look no further for investments, but to put his money into the harvester company. When, two years later, the books showed that Deering had doubled his money, he asked to be taken into the business as a partner. By the next year, poor health caused Gammon to call for Deering to move to Chicago and take over management of the business. In 1880, Gammon sold out to Deering.

By 1890, McCormick and Deering were leaders in the harvesting industry. Deering, by now getting on in years, proposed, in 1897, to sell out to Cyrus McCormick, Jr., but McCormick was unable to raise the cash. Vigorous competition resumed, with Deering continuing to gain on McCormick's leadership. Then, in 1902, the two leaders, along with five other companies, merged to form the International Harvester Company. William Deering died at age eighty-seven.

While the component companies of International Harvester had pioneered the grain harvesting industry, not one of the five had produced threshing machines. Apparently thinking that the two lines were not compatible, International Harvester made no effort to become a full-line supplier until 1909. At that time, it acquired marketing rights to the Belle City

A unique combination ad circa 1918 that advocates the use of the Fordson tractor with the Belle City-New Racine thresher. The ad is especially unusual in light of the fact that Belle City was part of International Harvester, as was McCormick-Deering, who made competing tractors. Tractor competition was not so severe until after 1924, when International Harvester's Farmall challenged the Fordson as "the world's most popular tractor."

Aultman-Taylor was once a leading manufacturer of American agricultural implements, from its 15-30 kerosene tractor to its New Century Thresher.

thresher, being made in Racine, Wisconsin, and the Little Giant thresher, being made by Heebner and Sons of Lansdale, Pennsylvania. Similar rights were obtained for the

Buffalo Pitts thresher in 1913. International Harvester successfully sold these wooden units until 1925, when the all-steel McCormick-Deering

threshers were introduced.

The Little Giant thresher was marketed under the name Sterling Thresher. For the 1911 harvest season, Sterling brought out an interesting variation: a Sterling thresher and an International Harvester gasoline engine for power, mounted on a wheeled chassis. This arrangement, according to company advertising, was ideal for the smaller farmer who did

The arrow in the above cut at figure 1 points to the lever by which the front end of lower sieve is raised or dropped for wheat or oats threshing without stopping the machine. The arrow at 2 points to lever by which the quantity of blast is regulated. The arrow at 3 indicates the lever by which the blast is directed to any part of the riddle desired. The lever at 4 operates the adjustable sieve. Figure 5 indicates the automatic oscillating wind stacker turn table. By turning the hand wheel at figure 6 the concaves may be raised or lowered to suit the requirements.

It will be readily seen by the above explanation how handy this separator is and how easy it is to adjust. For fast threshing, perfect cleaning and grain saving qualities it is unequaled. Its patented alternating oscillating agitating racks completely break, shake and tear apart the straw eight times before it reaches the windstacker. Our catalog will explain.

THE BIG BROTHER OF THE BAKER ENGINE

THE LITTLE ENGINE WITH THE BIG PULL

Each of the above engines is equipped with the Baker Reverse Valve Gear. This reverse gear is doing the same service for both, making possible increased efficiency and power with less fuel and water. The mere fact that forty-seven leading railroads of the United States and Mexico have adopted this Baker Reverse should be sufficient proof that there is truth in what we claim for it.

Description of our engines and separators in detail may be had by sending for our new 1911 catalog.

The A. D. Baker Co., Swanton, Ohio

not want to invest in a steam rig or rely on the neighborhood threshing ring. As a bonus, the engine could be used for other farm chores.

The A. D. Baker Company was established in 1903 around its patented steam engine reversing-valve gear. The company went on to manufacture a line of larger threshing machines especially for the custom threshing trade, the largest being a 36 × 62 machine requiring 60hp to operate.

The Golden Age of the Threshers

Arise and thresh, O daughter of Zion . . .
— Micah 4:13

The first third of the twentieth century, up until the crash of 1929, saw unparalleled burgeoning prosperity in the farm implement business. Political conditions in both the United States and Canada were conducive to agricultural expansion, the western prairies were opened up for settlement, and high immigration provided the people to make it all happen.

The rapidly expanding railroad system also fueled the engine of progress. Working hand-in-pocket with the governments of the two countries, the new rail system made populating the western lands practical. Not only did the system provide transportation, but perhaps even more important, the railroad work gave the impoverished immigrant a grub-stake in the new land.

Technology also contributed to the good times. Development of steel alloys in the late 1800s allowed the redesign of most farm tools and implements, and made ball and roller bearings available in place of bushings. J. I. Case introduced the first all-steel threshing machine in 1904.

The giant implement companies were expanding by leaps and bounds. From 1901 until 1911, Massey-Harris, for example, expanded two-and-a-half

Handle Your Threshing and Hulling for 1914 the "SCIENTIFIC" Way!

Scientific

————Built by————

Illinois Thresher Company
(INC.)

SYCAMORE — De Kalb County — ILLINOIS

WM. N. RUMELY, President and Gen'l Mgr.   P. B. McINTYRE, Secretary and Treasurer

A huller for clover and alfalfa MUST have **three times the chaffing capacity** of a grain separator; MUST have a **rasp cylinder** to tear off the felty pods that enclose the seed, otherwise a great portion of seed will necessarily go into the chaff pile—no **separator** can do this with an **attachment** of concaves, as it lacks essential parts.

The "SCIENTIFIC" has as great chaffing capacity as the **large hullers**; has a **larger** Rasp Cylinder through which all seed must pass before final separation; and has a **large recleaner** which puts the seed in marketable shape as it comes from the machine. The "SCIENTIFIC" WAY of hulling is the perfect way.

In grain threshing, the "SCIENTIFIC" WAY is to use the same great chaffing surface, which prevents overloading of the sieve shoe and insures clean, thorough work.

This machine **is** a successful SCIENTIFIC COMBINATION THRESHER AND HULLER!

COME AND SEE—or write for descriptive circular and information.

Previous page
This beautifully maintained 1945 Oliver Red River Special, owned by Don Elliott of Kingston, Illinois, makes an annual appearance at the Northern Illinois Steam Power Club's Sycamore Show. The Red River boasted ball bearings on the cylinders and all-steel construction. Dale Thompson is the thresherman and George White is pitching bundles.

William N. Rumely was instrumental in founding the Illinois Thresher Company in 1914, after the reorganized M. Rumely and Company was taken over by his nephew, Dr. Edward A. Rumely. This ad shows the features of the Illinois Thresher Company's product, called the "Scientific."

A well-preserved original logo on a 1920 Huber thresher. Called the Supreme, the Huber was one of the most popular Midwestern threshers.

times. A great part of the European immigration was put to work by the implement factories.

With all this political, technological, and economic activity came the twentieth-century Midwest grain farmer. His way of life revolved around hard work, self-sacrifice, strong family ties, and a spirit of political involvement. He exemplified a sense of

Charles Doty, thresherman from Princeton, Illinois, watches as the grain weigher-counter does its job at the Franklin Grove, Illinois, Living History Antique Equipment Show. Note the smoke from the Case steamer, which is providing the motivating power to the 28 × 46 Huber thresher.

independence on a large scale, but of interdependence on a neighborhood scale. He was perhaps short on formal education, but long on "know-how."

The Twentieth-Century Threshing Scene

By 1900, grain farming across the United States and Canada was big business, but was done mostly by small operators. In the Great Plains states and provinces, and in California, there were, however, some large wheat farms. In either case, threshing was one of the most important tasks of the year.

The entire year's crop—the product of a year's labor—was put through the threshing machine in one day. In this brief time, one-fifth of the total human labor and one-tenth of the horse labor required to produce the crop was expended.

The big thresher was Queen of the Harvest up through World War II. As those who have lived through a good part of that time will attest, there were good times, but also turbulent times, given the Depression, the drought and Dust Bowl of the thirties, the population of the western states and provinces, rural electrification, and two world wars. The farm machinery business had never settled down since the great harvester wars of the previous century.

Because of the size of a thresher, sales at the beginning of the century tended to be fairly regional, despite the availability of good rail transport. As time went on, though, the larger and stronger companies began to amalgamate and to acquire the weaker.

The machines themselves also changed to mostly metal and all-metal construction. Feeders and stackers were virtually standard equipment, and almost no one used horse-powered treadmills.

Custom Threshing

At no time throughout the year did farm men work at such high tension as

Belt trouble: the nemesis of the thresher. Thresherman Charles Doty re-makes a drive belt. Devices such as miniature door hinges are clamped onto each end of the belt, and then a pin is inserted to hold the ends together. Getting new belts the exact length required is not an easy task.

A 1915 Case 50hp steam traction engine, owned for six years by Clyde Bearrows of Rochelle, Illinois. That's not an OSHA inspector checking for belt guards, but Bearrows' assistant, Don Vogeler, also of Rochelle.

at threshing time. It was a period that demanded total involvement by men, women, and children big enough to help. Help was exchanged throughout the neighborhood. Because of the possibility of rain, the job was always done at top speed.

The straw flies from the wind stacker on a lovely July afternoon at the 22nd Annual Stephenson County (Illinois) Old Fashioned Threshing Show & Antique Display. A big Keck-Gonnerman Indiana Special fills the air with straw. A rare F-30 Farmall pulls the bundle wagon.

The thresherman atop the separator was the boss of the outfit and responsible for the clean threshing of the grain. At his signal, the driving engine's speed would be adjusted to the best for that particular machine. This is a scene from the 1991 Stephenson County Old Fashioned Threshing Show, held at Freeport, Illinois. The separator is a Keck-Gonnerman.

Developed during this time was a phenomenon known as custom threshing. It was a variation of the threshing ring, described earlier, where the rig owner went beyond his own neighborhood, following the harvest north. The custom thresher usually provided at least part of the crew: men to run the engine and thresher. Custom threshing was an institution in rural America for several decades. To many a young boy, the lot of the thresher was the pinnacle of ambition. The life of travel, the romance of steam power, and the mystique of the stranger fascinated both boys and (to the consternation of the farmer) girls.

During their heyday, the ranks of custom threshers rose to 75,000 grease-besmirched, tobacco-chewing, dedicated individuals. The way of life of the custom thresher was not easy—long hours, home-life sacrificed, mostly sleeping outside—all for modest-at-best financial reward. Most came back, year after year, lured on by public esteem, their love of machinery, the satisfaction of a job well done, and the matchless food served by the farm women.

Feeding the Threshers

No conversation with old-time threshers at gatherings today will be complete until the threshing dinner is discussed. Today's young people probably wonder about the expression "eat like a bunch of threshers," but it was a scene rivaled only by that of the logging-camp dining rooms in the north. And, as in the case of the logging camps, it was the good food that attracted the help; without good food, no inducement was adequate.

The women began the preparation days ahead of time. The best places had

59

He fed the SAME Belle City THRESHER *for* 25 YEARS

This is but one of the letters from thousands of satisfied Belle City Users.

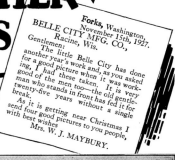

Forks, Washington,
November 15th, 1927.
BELLE CITY MFG. CO.,
Racine, Wis.
Gentlemen:
The little Belle City has done another year's work and, as you asked for a good picture when it was working, I had these taken. It is very good of the men too—the old gentleman who stands in front has fed it for twenty-five years without a single break.
As it is getting near Christmas I send four good pictures to you people, with best wishes
Mrs. W. J. MAYBURY.

YOU have doubtless read and heard about many threshers, and we know that it is hard to choose from so many good ones. But if you will carefully post yourself on the Belle City, you will see, without a question, it is a thresher which really "has the edge" on all of them in many ways.

Mrs. Maybury's letter will convince you of Belle City durability, and remember that today, the Belle City is an all-steel thresher, with full Timken Roller Bearing equipment and Alemite-Zerk lubrication—a better, finer, even more durable thresher than the one which is serving Mrs. Maybury so well.

Today—Better Than Ever

The Belle City Thresher has been a pioneer, a pathfinder, and is still a leader in meeting today's conditions and requirements. Belle City was building individual size threshers way back when the custom thresher was having its day. Our small sizes are not big ones cut down to little ones—they are designed from tip to tip for small tractor power. They are made good to stay good—guaranteed against defective material for the life of the thresher.

Belle City Threshers are built roomy for large capacity. They have the longest grate surface of any threshers of equal size, and full width of the thresher. This gives you 90 to 98 per cent separation at the grate. The counterbalanced, four-section, extra-capacity straw rack means one-third more agitation, more complete separation. Belle City Threshers pay for themselves in grain saved. Get our free book and compare Belle City specifications and features with other threshers.

More for Your Money

The Belle City will really save you engine power, save grain, save time and save money. Compare Belle City prices as well as quality. Fast, clean, thorough separation; light running, freedom from vibration, high standard of construction, low cost of upkeep, are all outstanding features of the Belle City and make it a profitable investment.

Belle City dealers are equipped to give you liberal terms.

Quality Products Since 1882

BELLE CITY BUILT

FOUR SIZES:
20x32
22x40
24x40
28x48

Get this FREE BOOK of Valuable Thresher Facts

Find out what 46 years of experience have taught Belle City about threshers. Find out what Belle City Threshers have done for other users throughout the country. Find out why the Belle City offers you more for less money. Mail the coupon today.

BELLE CITY MFG. CO.
Dept. 10   RACINE WISCONSIN   2-28

Mail Coupon Today for FREE Book

BELLE CITY MFG. CO.
Dept. 10   Racine, Wis.
Send me your new free book of Thresher Facts and complete description of new 1928 Belle City Threshers. I raise ....acres of grain and seeds. I have a............ Tractor. Am interested in....................size thresher.

Name ....

Town ....

F. R. D. .... State ....

This ad for the Belle City thresher appeared in February 1928. Although not mentioned in the ad, Belle City was part of International Harvester Corporation. Belle City specialized in smaller machines for individual farmers or small threshing rings.

three, or perhaps four, kinds of meat on the table: ham, roast pork or beef, chicken, and meatballs. There were always two or three kinds of vegetables, plus mashed or boiled potatoes and gravy, and, of course, the inevitable crock of oven-baked beans. Fresh-picked lettuce and cucumbers in vinegar were regulars, as were all manner of pickles. Rounding out the meal were fresh, home-baked bread and biscuits, over which you could pour gravy or spread home-churned butter and blackberry jam.

But dessert was the *piece de resistance*. Several kinds of pies (cut in fourths)—usually apple and berry and rhubarb—along with big slabs of cheese graced the table. Sometimes, strawberry shortcake with whipped cream was also served. It was all washed down with gallons of hot coffee.

At least in the Midwest, this meal, dinner, was at noon. The help arrived after the dew had dried, and left for home and their own dairy chores before supper. When a custom thresher was employed, the host was obliged to provide breakfast and supper for him and his crew of four or five. These meals

were usually no more than the usual family fare. Supper would be leftovers from dinner, but in place of the pie, which was usually gone, there would be blueberry, blackberry, raspberry, apple, or rhubarb (pie plant) sauce.

It's not hard to see that providing such a meal, for up to twenty-five hungry men, was a costly proposition. While it was great for cementing relationships in the community, and offered fellowship and a remarkable feast to celebrate the harvest, it was a considerable part of the cost of the harvest. Besides the obvious costs were the risks of a rainy day, breakdowns, or just optimistic scheduling throwing off the timing. Most farms of the period did not have refrigeration, so the waste of substance (and human effort) could be horrendous if no one showed up for the meal on the day anticipated. As farms got bigger and more mechanized, the

Leveling the rig; the thresher must be level laterally, and slightly down in the back, for proper function. Joe Yanich, Phillips, Wisconsin, digs holes in the sod, into which the wheels will be rolled. The holes also keep the rig from rolling toward the tractor and loosening the drive belt.

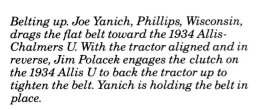

Belting up. Joe Yanich, Phillips, Wisconsin, drags the flat belt toward the 1934 Allis-Chalmers U. With the tractor aligned and in reverse, Jim Polacek engages the clutch on the 1934 Allis U to back the tractor up to tighten the belt. Yanich is holding the belt in place.

Don and Kathleen Onchuck's White Pine
Dairy, outside of Phillips, Wisconsin; the
thresher has been spotted and belted up.
Here, Joe Yanich stretches out the wind
stacker chute toward the spot desired for the
straw pile. "It's ready to run," says Joe
Yanich of Phillips, Wisconsin. The 1948 Belle
City thresher is a 22 × 40 size, which
provides a good load for the Allis-Chalmers
Model U.

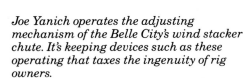

Joe Yanich operates the adjusting
mechanism of the Belle City's wind stacker
chute. It's keeping devices such as these
operating that taxes the ingenuity of rig
owners.

Jim Polacek applies belt dressing, which improves traction and keeps the belts supple. Polacek is the owner of Polacek Implement in Phillips, Wisconsin, a Ford tractor and implement dealership.

Molly, on the left, and Mary Lou, a team of registered Belgian mares, are not unnerved by their close proximity to the singing flatbelt. Driving the team is their owner, Dennis Mathison, a CPA from Phillips, Wisconsin. Don Onchuck and his dad, Bill, pitch the bundles.

The engineer's point of view, as Bill Onchuck and Phil Klaar pitch the last of the bundles into the Hart-Carter feeder. Bill Polacek, left, mans the bagger, while Joe Yanich takes his place atop the rig. In the background are the buildings of Onchuck's White Pine Dairy; in the foreground is Jim Polacek's 1951 Ford 8N.

equitable sharing of labor, and the threshing dinner, became more difficult. Switching from the traditional method to the newfangled combine became more attractive.

Combines Take Over

Contemporary with the rapid development of the reaper and thresher, Hiram Moore of Kalamazoo County, Michigan, built the first

"successful" combine. Short Midwest summers and small grain fields, however, did not lend themselves to the use of this gigantic machine. Also, the requirement for up to twenty horses for propulsion and ten to twelve men did not relieve the farmer of his major problems. Finally, the risk associated with reliance on one unproven machine for the entire harvest was more than most farmers would consider.

Bill Polacek handles the grain bags. The bagging attachment is the bifurcated downshcot with an empty bag attached to one leg. Bill has just removed a full bag from the other, after flipping the diverter gate at the junction to fill the empty bag. By the time it's full, Bill will have tied another empty bag to the other leg.

Nevertheless, the idea of a machine that would complete the harvest in one operation was intriguing. Southern-hemisphere wheat was said to ripen faster than that in the north, to the extent that grain heads were likely to fall off in the process of cutting and shocking. Thus, there was a real need in Australia and Argentina for a faster method of harvesting. Massey-Harris, with worldwide operations by the turn of the century, perfected its Reaper-Thresher No. 1 for these conditions, but found it worked well in the north as well. It was the first requiring less horse- and manpower, cutting the harvesting requirements by two-thirds.

The advent of the combine was still delayed to a great extent by World War I

and the Great Depression, but especially in the west, it had largely taken over by 1930. In the Midwest, it was mostly just an idea until 1938, when Allis-Chalmers brought out its famous All-Crop Harvester.

The All-Crop stemmed from a revolutionary cylinder design by a California inventor named Robert Fleming, using wire bristles rather than cast-iron teeth. The Fleming invention also called for a cylinder width the same as that of the cutter. In 1930, Allis-Chalmers bought the shop rights to the invention and announced imminent production. At the time, Allis-Chalmers was negotiating for the acquisition of Advance-Rumely, and this

announcement may have been for the purpose of speeding up that process. Advance-Rumely was folded into Allis-Chalmers in 1931, coinciding with the development of the lightweight, inexpensive All-Crop. Problems with the bristles breaking off and finding their way into animal food was reminiscent of the days of the wire binders, and so the cylinder had to be redesigned.

The new design featured diagonal rubber-coated bars instead of the bristles. Other innovative construction practices, such as vee-belt drives and spot-weld assemblies resulted in a 3000lb machine which was power takeoff operated by the tractor pulling it. Now, finally, harvesting a moderately sized farm was a one-man job. Other manufacturers soon jumped on the bandwagon, and power takeoff combines became the norm for a short time before self-propelled combines took the field. The details and traumas of combine development are another story, however, beyond the scope of this book.

Threshing Machines: How They Worked

The twentieth-century grain thresher was a wonderfully efficient machine. The thresher not only threshed, separated, and cleaned the grain, but weighed it and delivered it to the bags, wagon, or granary, while the straw was delivered to the stack or mow. All this took place in about thirty seconds from the time the bundle was placed into the feeder. With the thresher, a man could accomplish more than thirty men could in the days of the flail, and the work was performed better and with less waste.

While there were many threshing machine brands, each with specific characteristics, the threshing operation was similar for them all. First, the kernels of grain were loosened from the straw by the cylinder and concaves, called the threshing apparatus. Then, the grain was separated from the straw

A good view of the bagging attachment in operation. Bill Polacek's hand is on the diverter control, which switches the grain from one bag to the next as the bags fill. A canvas tarp is used to collect spillage.

by the straw rack or, in some machines, the straw walkers. This was called the separating apparatus. Finally, the grain was cleaned and separated from the chaff and other refuse in the cleaning apparatus.

Threshers were typically measured by their cylinder and separator width. Thus the Minneapolis Thresher 44×72 had a cylinder 44in wide and a separator 72in wide.

As the grain bundles are fed into the machine, they first come in contact with the cylinder and concaves. The cylinder teeth strike the grain with sufficient force to shatter the kernels from the head. The velocity of the rotating cylinder is imparted to the grain and straw so that when they come in contact with the stationary concave teeth, which project between the cylinder teeth, they receive another blow of great force, further knocking the grain from the heads. For smaller grains, such as wheat, oats, or barley, a tip speed of the cylinder teeth of about 6200fpm (feet per minute) brings good results. Thus, machines with larger-diameter cylinders must run the cylinder slower to get the same effect. Driving-pulley diameter and engine operating speed are also important factors: too slow, and threshing will not be complete; too high, and the grain will be cracked and the straw will be broken into short pieces that get through the racks and make cleaning difficult. Occasionally, tough grain can be threshed better by using a slightly higher-than-normal speed.

Cylinder and concave teeth are, on more recent models, drop-forged and hardened to resist wear and breakage. Corrugated teeth are sometimes used, especially for hard-to-thresh grains, such as "Turkey Red" wheat. On these later machines, the cylinders generally run on ball bearings, but roller and journal bearings were also used, especially on earlier machines.

After the kernels have been removed from the heads, they must be separated from the straw. This operation takes place in the separating members and straw rack.

The grain-and-straw mixture comes out of the cylinder/concave at a high velocity. It first passes through a beater which prevents it from becoming caught in the cylinder, directing it

downward and backward onto the rack. Upon reaching the rack, its motion is retarded to about 100fpm. The kernels are allowed to fall through the straw and rack slats and onto grates, or sieves, below; the long straws cannot get through. This is where brands of

The harvester was the forerunner of the combine, which was basically a powered harvester. Allis-Chalmers' All-Crop was a pioneer in the field.

Massey-Harris' harvester featured a 6ft wide clipper that was driven off of your tractor's power takeoff.

machines differ: some rely on agitation of the straw rack to get the grain through the straw so that it can drop onto the grates; some use "fluffers" to lift and drop the straw; and some use narrow racks with an alternating rotary motion, like that of a man walking on a pair of snowshoes, called straw walkers.

The function of the rack section is to transport the straw to the back of the machine, where the stacker takes over, and in the process, to agitate in such a way that the grain can fall through to the sieves below.

After the grain has been separated from the straw, it is mixed with large quantities of chaff and refuse which have passed through the racks. The function of the cleaning apparatus is to separate the grain from this and to dispose of the refuse. This is done by passing the uncleaned grain over a series of holes, or sieves, through which a current of air is forced. The combination of sieves and screens is usually called the "shoe." Later machines use sieves that may be adjusted to the type of grain being processed. The grain is supposed to fall through the sieve, while chaff, etc., is carried away by the airflow. To further clean the grain, most machines also use screens in the shoe. The screen mesh is smaller than the grain and its purpose is to support the grain while sand, weed seeds and the like, fall through to the ground.

The airflow, or fan blast, is an important part of the process. Its function is the same as that of the fan in the old-time fanning mill. The flow must be just right to carry away everything lighter than the grain kernels. It must be even over the entire sieve. Flow is regulated by fan blinds, which must be adjusted to get the desired results. If threshing conditions change, readjustment is necessary. It is also important to feed bundles into the machine at an even rate, or if that is not possible, to check the adjustment of the blinds.

Unthreshed heads and all trash that is too coarse to fall through the sieve and too heavy to be blown out by the blast are called tailings. Tailings are conveyed to the tailings elevator and are thereby carried back to the front of the machine and injected into the cylinder for reprocessing. The amount of tailings is a good indication of how the rest of the machine is performing. Too much being re-injected into the cylinder is an indication that adjustments are needed somewhere in the machine.

Devices used for taking the processed grain from the shoe are called grain handlers. They consist of a series of augers and conveyors which carry clean grain through a weigher/counter and to either a grain wagon or to a bagger. Baggers use a bifurcated duct with a shutter control, so that grain is directed first to one bag and then to the second while the first is removed, tied, and replaced.

The power required to thresh is extremely variable. It is also difficult to compare machines, as some companies are conservative and some are sporty. As a general rule of thumb, a basic threshing machine with a feeder, weigher, and wind stacker requires about one horsepower for each three bushels of wheat threshed per hour. Simpler machines required less power than the more complex, and of course, larger machines require more power than smaller. The rate of threshing and the kind and condition of the grain also affect the power requirement. Thus, if hard-to-thresh wheat is being processed, slower feeding might be required than for oats, if the prime mover is power-limited.

Power required for various attachments is as follows: a feeder with bundle cutter, speed governor, and straw governor takes from two to five horsepower, depending on the size of the machine; a wind stacker requires three to eight horsepower. Grain handlers usually take less than one horsepower.

Engine power is transmitted to various parts of the thresher by pulleys and belts, sprockets and chains, cranks and pitman arms, and, to a smaller extent, gears. Of these, the belt and pulley were the most common.

Pulleys were often crowned to make alignment less critical. The Rockwood fiber pulley was much better than plain steel or wood for traction under all conditions. Threshers were warned, in the event of rain, to remove all belts and place them in a dry place, because of loss of traction due to a wet belt. Operators were also advised to have an extra set of belts handy to prevent downtime in the event of belt breakage or loss of traction.

Leather belts have a "hair side," which should be against the pulley for best results. They can become dry and hard; if that happens, they can be restored by soaking in neat's-foot oil.

Rubber belts were also used, which didn't require dressings. Care was

The arrival of the self-propelled combine marked the end of the thresher, and again J. I. Case led the way. This ad shows Case's PTO-driven 77 harvester and its new 150 combine.

Jim Polacek's Belle City thresher uses a Hart-Carter feeder. The feeder was optional equipment. It consisted of the conveyor and the bundle cutters. It also contained an apparatus that regulated the flow of grain into the threshing cylinder to prevent choking or clogging.

needed to prevent oil or any sticky substance from coming in contact with the belt, as the coating could be easily damaged.

Canvas belts were also used, especially for the main drive. They came in four-, five-, and six-ply

Trademark logo on Jim Polacek's Belle City thresher. These threshers were made in Racine, Wisconsin, the same town that produced Case threshers. Belle City was owned by International Harvester after 1909.

STRAW
SHAKERS
160
RPM

The Red River Special thresher was made first by the famous Nichols & Shepard threshing machine pioneers. Later, the line was taken over by the Oliver Farm Equipment Sales Company.

thicknesses. The greater the number of plies, the larger the pulley diameter required. A six-ply belt, for example, required a pulley diameter of 12in.

The length of the belt used for the main drive depended on whether the power was from a steam or internal combustion engine. The fire hazard associated with a steam engine, especially when wood or straw was burned, made as long a belt as possible desirable. Thus, belts of 160ft were not uncommon. Shorter belts were recommended for a gas tractor, as this allowed one man to look after both ends of the outfit. The weight of the longer belt also added greatly to pulley

traction. With the giant steam engine, it was difficult to achieve the desired belt tension on soft ground, as the machine resisted small, well-controlled movements. Thus, the weight of a long belt was a help. For the smaller internal combustion tractor, with its slippable clutch and separate braking system, exact belt tension could be achieved with a shorter belt.

Generally, drive belts were twisted. This had a damping effect on the long

Previous page
The Northern Illinois Steam Power Club holds its Sycamore Show on the Marshall Taylor Farm, about fifty miles west of Chicago, for four days early in August each year. The thresher is a 1945 Oliver Red River Special, owned by Don Elliot of Kingston, Illinois.

The 22 × 36 Oliver Red River Special spews straw at the 1991 Sycamore Show, under the watchful eye of thresherman Dale Thompson. In the background, providing the motive power, is a pristine 1936 Minneapolis-Moline Twin City Model J tractor, owned by Avery Stevens of St. Charles, Illinois.

Belt too short? Splice in a piece. This view clearly shows how belt ends are hooked together.

The object in feeding a thresher is to keep a steady stream of bundles in the conveyor, kernel-end first. Two pitchers need to develop a cadence where one is spearing a bundle while the other is dropping his in.

The two most common problems for the novice pitcher are standing on the bundle you are trying to pick up and having the bundle hang up on the fork just enough to drop short of the conveyor.

belt and helped keep it from jumping off the pulleys. The main consideration, however, was direction of rotation. In some cases with an internal combustion engine, a twist could not be used because the driver could not turn the thresher in the right direction. Steam engines could generally run in either direction, however.

This ad from the Hart Grain Weigher Company features two of its products which, it claims, can save you $40 per day—no small amount in 1910. The wing carrier allowed the threshing machine to be fed from both sides and either from the bundle wagon or from the ground. The thresher rack was a "self-unloading" bundle wagon. The trailing rope was connected to a fixed object, pulling the load out of the wagon to the

ground near the wing carrier, as the wagon continued on its way. Thus, the wagon was quickly back in the field picking up another load, reducing the number of wagons, teams, and drivers required.

The Dentler Bagger was an upscale type of patented recording bagger that could be specified for any kind of thresher. They were popular around the turn of the century.

Palmer Fossum of Northfield, Minnesota, surveys his domain from the top of his 1941 Woods Bros. Hummingbird thresher, built in Des Moines, Iowa. Michael Dregni of St. Paul, Minnesota, mans the bagger. Michael Dapper of Minneapolis, Minnesota, pitches a bundle into the feeder. By 1941, when this Wood Bros. thresher was built, the threshing machine was a more-or-less mature item. Once the grain was pitched into the feeder, it was handled by conveyors, elevators, augers, and blowers until the kernels came out in the bagger and the straw and chaff came out the wind stacker chute. The thresherman (in this case Palmer Fossum, oilcan in hand) kept a watchful eye on the process, ready to make adjustments at a moment's notice.

Getting all the flat drive belts on a thresher could sometimes be as much of a problem as threading a movie projector. If it began to rain, the thresherman quickly shut down and pulled all the belts off and got them to a dry place. It's embarrassing, when installing the belts, to forget to twist one, which results in an auger running backwards, or the like.

Previous page
Larry Holt, and his newly restored 1946
Ford-Ferguson 2N, provide the driving power
for Palmer Fossum's 1941 Wood Bros.
thresher. Wood Bros. was in 1941 owned by
Ford. Both Larry Holt and Palmer Fossum
are from Northfield, Minnesota.

The Wood Bros. threshing machine was
tradenamed the Hummingbird, to suggest
quiet-running and light weight.

The afternoon Minnesota sun lights up the
Wood Bros. logo on Palmer Fossum's 1941
thresher.

Palmer Fossum observes the effluent of the
tailings elevator (the pipe running
diagonally up the side of the machine), while
Michael Dregni attaches another bag to the
bagger. Using bags, rather than running the
grain directly into a wagon, was often done
before self-unloading wagons came on the
scene.

Previous page
An afternoon cloud silhouettes the end of the
wind stacker chute as Michael Dregni and
Palmer Fossum (with the hat) attend to their
duties.

In the late forties, thresher manufacturers
began mounting their own brand of feeder
as standard equipment. Here is an example
by Belle City.

Previous page
Flat belt repair. Palmer Fossum trims the
belt coupling to the width of the belt.

The wind stacker chute could be manually adjusted in elevation, azimuth, and angle of discharge from its base. During operation, a drive gear could be engaged to automatically sweep the chute back and forth to make a semi-circular straw pile.

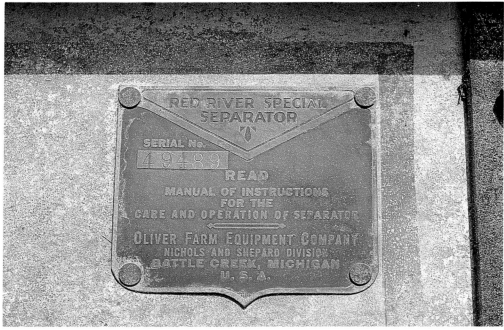

RED RIVER SPECIAL
SEPARATOR

SERIAL No.
4 94 89
READ
MANUAL OF INSTRUCTIONS
FOR THE
CARE AND OPERATION OF SEPARATOR

OLIVER FARM EQUIPMENT COMPANY
NICHOLS AND SHEPARD DIVISION
BATTLE CREEK, MICHIGAN
U.S.A.

The serial number plate of an Oliver Red River Special thresher. The number is 19180.

A once-proud name logo on the tailings elevator of this Oliver Red River Special now shows the effect of years in the sun and weather. Often, threshers were too big for farmers to get them under cover.

The wind stacker nozzle could be adjusted for angle of discharge, as well as rotational angle, left and right.

*The No. 2 Champion, by Ellis Keystone,
shows the wood craftsmanship apparent in
nineteenth-century threshers. This
particular thresher is from about 1890.*

A big Minneapolis 27-42 cross-engine tractor drives a Frick thresher, circa 1937. This farmer should have enough straw to last for a while.

A new Frick thresher in 1937, with the grain bagger in operation.

Next page
The drive engines brought in at thresherees are often of great interest to the spectators. A thresher makes a good steady load against which to test an engine.

HART-PARR

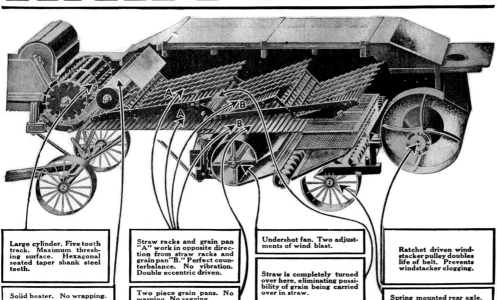

Large cylinder. Five tooth track. Maximum threshing surface. Hexagonal seated taper shank steel teeth.

Straw racks and grain pan "A" work in opposite direction from straw racks and grain pan "B." Perfect counterbalance. No vibration. Double eccentric driven.

Undershot fan. Two adjustments of wind blast.

Ratchet driven windstacker pulley doubles life of belt. Prevents windstacker clogging.

Solid beater. No wrapping.

Two piece grain pans. No warping. No sagging.

Straw is completely turned over here, eliminating possibility of grain being carried over in straw.

Spring mounted rear axle.

Hart-Parr Threshing Outfit Makes Threshing Easy

All threshers are made to thresh—all will do the work under good conditions. But the separator you want is the separator that has the greatest capacity and does the best work under every condition—the separator that is easiest to handle and adjust, the separator that is well made and has long life.

The Hart-Parr "Money-Maker" has hardwood sills. It is thoroughly reinforced from deck to axles. Every joint is a tight fit. No twists or bends—it is a sturdy, durable separator.

The cylinder is a 15-bar large cylinder equipped with steel teeth with hexagonal tapered shanks. These teeth withstand the most severe tests. A loose tooth in the Hart-Parr "Money-Maker" is rare.

The Hart-Parr "Money-Maker" is double belted and double eccentric driven. This insures smooth running, eliminates side strain and means longer life. One-half of the straw racks and grain pan is balanced against the other half.

Think of the value of these features!—perfect counterbalance, no vibration, long life, no grain pan warping or sagging out of shape.

The capacity of the Hart-Parr "Money-Maker" is limited only to the number of pitchers at the feeder. It has ample straw clearance. At the center of the racks the straw is completely inverted, insuring thorough separation and eliminating carry-over.

Our ratchet windstacker drive pulley equalizes the difference in speed between the cylinder and the windstacker. This saves your windstacker belt and prevents clogging of the windstacker.

All adjustments are on the outside of the Hart-Parr "Money-Maker" within easy reach. All oiling is done from the outside. The undershot fan with two windboard adjustments means sure and thorough cleaning under all conditions. The Hart-Parr "Money-Maker" is equipped with adjustable sieve and riddles, with belt reel and belt pulley guides—at the same price, and without extra charge. The feeder is a solid steel feeder—no chance to clog, no chance to warp.

It is a pleasure to thresh with the Hart-Parr "Money-Maker." You can make more money with it. With a Hart-Parr "Money-Maker" you have a long-lived machine as well as a very efficient and easily adjusted separator.

Write at once for detailed catalog, giving us the size engine for which you want a separator.

Hart-Parr Tractors

The "Old Reliable" is just what the name implies. The Hart-Parr "Old Reliables" have served farmers for years. Hundreds are in use. Not only will they thresh and plow, but they are reliable, economical, kerosene burning tractors for road grading, hauling, field work, etc. We founded the tractor industry and our tractors are the result of years of experience in building tractor leaders.

Hart-Parr tractors are made in three sizes:

The "Old Reliable"—"Our 60."
The "Oil King—35."
The "New Hart-Parr"—Three Plow.

Write for full information. Special inducements to dealers handling large sales.

THE HART-PARR COMPANY
558 Lawler St.   Charles City, Iowa

Hart-Parr made one of the best wooden threshers before being taken over by Oliver. One of their main features was the inversion of the straw between the straw racks, supposedly eliminating the possibility of the grain being carried out with the straw.

A Minneapolis 22 × 36 thresher shows its stuff at the 1991 Dodge County, Wisconsin, thresheree. The Minneapolis Threshing Machine Company was located in Hopkins, Minnesota.

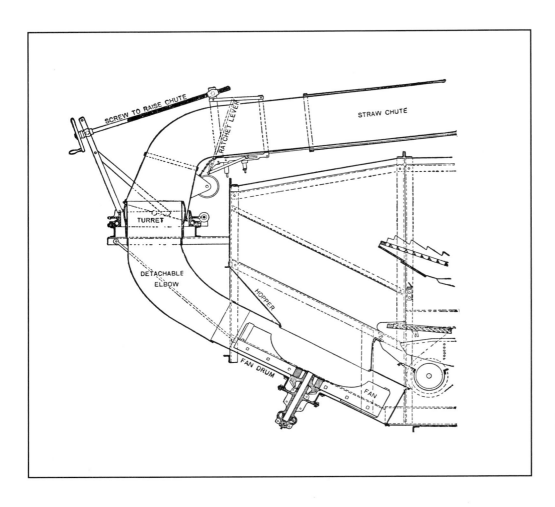

Sectional view of a wind stacker.

The 1991 Dodge County, Wisconsin, theresheree brought together many machines and threshermen, young and old.

The wind stacker drive belt on an old
Minneapolis brand thresher. It transmits
about 20hp at full speed.

Fond du Lac, Wisconsin, thresherman Bob Cofeen, checks out a Minneapolis thresher at the Dodge County Antique Power Club's show near Beaver Dam, Wisconsin.

A forties' Marshall steel threshing machine on rubber tires with a diesel Field Marshall Series III tractor. The owner of the thresher is W. Brent & Son, Callington, Cornwall. Photographed at the Marshall exhibit at the Great Dorset Steam Fair.

Previous page
Clayton & Shuttleworth of Lincoln, England. Built in 1896; the company had already produced more than 25,000 threshing machines since they started in 1842. This model was originally horse drawn and is now restored to good working order. Owner: A. M. Smith of North Cadbury, Yeovil, Somerset. Photographed at the Great Dorset Steam Fair.

Clayton & Shuttleworth has a 42in drum, being fed by Jack Wake of Wincanton, Somerset.

Clayton & Shuttleworth forty-two-inch drum and in-front hatch removed to show the 'Walkers' that pass the crop forwards. Clayton and Shuttleworth were building 16ft combine harvesters powered by an auxiliary engine in 1932.

Marshall built in 1943 at Gainsborough with a fifty-four-inch drum. Used for many years by Robert Thorne, Ltd., threshing contractors of Verwood, Dorset. Present owner: A. Phillips of Witchampton, Wimbourne. Powered by Marshall traction serial number 51025 of 7hp TE built in 1908.

The engine named 'Margaret' worked all its
life in Spalding, Lincolnshire, and traveled
600 miles a year among farms. Owner: M. S.
Parratt, who used to work for the Marshall
Company in Gainsborough, Lincolnshire.

Marshall threshing machine of the early forties, driven by a 1949 Field Marshall Series III tractor belonging to G. Munday of Shaftsbury, Dorset. The thresher is owned by Frith & Son of Shillingstone, Dorset.

Ransomes, Simms & Jefferies threshing machine built in 1944 in Ipswich, England, with 36in drum. Designed as a lightweight unit for farmers with 250 acres of crops. Owned by G. J. Romanes of Portesham, near Weymouth, Dorset.

He also owns the pretty Wallis & Steevens traction engine that is powering the thresher. Built in 1902 producing 3nhp and called 'Goliath,' it worked in a Brick and Tile Works until World War II, when it was kept for preservation. The Wallis & Steevens traction engines used their patent 'expansion' valve gear, which was designed to give economy when driving threshing machines on the belt.

Working with the Ransomes, Simms & Jefferies thresher is a 1948 Ross Junior baler built in Lanark, Scotland. Owned by J. Hatchard of Titchfield, Hampshire. Powering the baler is a John Deere Model A of 1948. Ransomes, Simms & Jefferies Co. is still in business today.

John Deere Model A of 1948 powering the Ross Junior baler of 1948. The Ransomes, Simms & Jefferies thresher in the background.

Foster medium threshing machine built in 1943 and fitted with Murch Reed comber. Bought by its present owner, B. C. Dibben, in the fifties and used continuously since. Today, besides being used at agricultural shows, it is worked commercially for three weeks every summer. The William Foster & Company, Ltd., of Lincoln, England, was best known for its traction engines.

The cast nameplate carries the picture of the tank built by Fosters for the British Army in World War I.

Belt joiner on the Foster's main feeder driving pulley.

Feeding crop into the Foster thresher; note correct thresher knife for quick cutting of bundle tie strings.

A Pool threshing machine built around 1900 as a fixed barn thresher and later converted to a portable by one of the last employees of W. H. Pool & Sons Company, Percy Brown. The Pool Company of Chipstable village in Somerset, England, made farm machinery. Like many other village and small-town farm companies in England and the United States, it copied standard designs of threshing machines. They built for local farmers, using mainly wood, as iron was expensive and foundries were a long distance away. These companies often employed only six workers but, with their lower overheads, could undercut the big manufacturers with price and personal service. Pool built its first threshing machine in 1847; it was horse drawn. Despite staying small, the Pool Company continued to build farm equipment up to 1956. William and Alfred Pool were brilliant engineers, but they liked the country too much and never moved to town to expand their business—like Jerome Case and John Deere.

The Pool thresher with 16in drum on show at the Somerset Rural Life Museum at Glastonbury, England. Here, David Walker, the Museum technician, hand feeds the crop into the drum.

Next page
The Pool thresher with Les Davies, who brings his 1958 International B450 to the Somerset Rural Life Museum for the belt power.

A 1928 Minneapolis 40x64 thresher owned by Maynard Petersen of Hampshire, Illinois, threshes oats at the Sycamore, Illinois, Thresheree. Power is being supplied by a 10-20 Minneapolis steamer, which according to the thresherman atop the machine, was a little short of power.

Rockwood marketed its fiber-based pulley as a replacement for the common metal pulley. As this 1938 ad stated, "Metal pulleys slip, Rockwood pulleys grip."

A freshly painted 1940 Oliver Red River Special threshes at the Sycamore, Illinois, show. Red River Specials were all steel by 1940, and employed ball bearings for the cylinder. The cylinder on this machine is 22in wide and the racks are 36in wide. It requires about 30hp for good operation, especially when ninety-four-year-old Ray Straw (with the red cap) is pitching bundles.

Val Hansen unfolds the Sattley Stacker with a hand crank. The stacker, mounted to her father's 1923 Case thresher, was power-swung 180deg from left to right in operation, making a semi-circular straw stack as much as 30ft high. It was able to stack straw from an entire day's threshing without resetting the machine.

for 67 YEARS THRESHER-WISE FARMERS HAVE DEMANDED BELLE CITY THRESHERS

The "He-Man" quality of Belle City Threshers has made them the favorite of thousands of farmers for three generations . . . and of farmers today who value a straw stack. Constant improvement has kept the Belle City modern to the minute . . . considered by many as *America's outstanding thresher value.* Here are some of the reasons:

1 **All-steel,** hot-riveted, modern construction . . . rugged, stand-up quality throughout.

2 **Full Timken Bearing Equipped** —Alemite Lubrication.

3 **Better Threshability** — Long grate surface, large straw rack capacity, more grain in the bin, cleaner grain, less labor, big capacity, light draft.

4 **A Size for Every Need**—22 x 40; 24 x 40; 28 x 48. Steel or rubber tires.

The Famous
JOLIET CORN SHELLER
Belle City Built

The original, and for many years, the only power corn sheller. All-steel, interlocked and welded frame and other distinctive features. Types for snapped and husked corn. Models in various sizes, stationary or portable, for individual or custom work.

•

The present demand for Belle City implements exceeds the supply, but Belle City dealers will do their best to serve you.

BELLE CITY also builds Corn Pickers, Castor Bean Hullers and Grain Elevators.

Belle City MANUFACTURING COMPANY, Racine, Wisconsin

116

Threshing Machine Specifications

. . . You shall not muzzle an ox when it is
treading out the grain . . .
—1 Corinthians 9:9

Trade Name	Weight (lb)	Cylinder Diameter	No. of Bars	Separator Length	Capacity (bu./hr.)	HP Required
Allis-Chalmers, Milwaukee, Wisconsin						
A-C Rumely 22×36	4,760	22	9	19'10"	100	20
A-C Rumely 28×46	7,410	21.7	12	26'	140	28
Avery Power Machinery Co., Peoria, Illinois						
Avery 22-36 Stl.	5,490	22	12	26'2"	NA	25
Avery 28-46 Stl.	6,000	22	12	26'2"	NA	35
Avery 32-52	6,900	22	12	26'2"	NA	40
A. D. Baker Co., Swanton, Ohio						
Baker 28×48	8,400	24	15	27'6"	NA	35
Baker 30×52	8,700	24	15	27'6"	NA	40
Baker 33×56	9,000	24	15	27'6"	NA	50
Baker 36×62	9,500	24	15	27'6"	NA	60
Banting Co., Toledo, Ohio						
Gryhnd 24×40	6,900	30	16	31'3"	NA	20
Gryhnd 28×48	7,400	30	16	31'3"	NA	30
Gryhnd 36×58	8,300	30	16	31'3"	NA	40
Belle City, Racine, Wisconsin						
21×33	4,170	19	9	24'7"	NA	20
25×41	5,900	23	12	29'6"	NA	25
29×49	7,075	23	12	30'8"	NA	30
Robert Bell, Seaforth, Ontario						
Imperial 24×36	5,800	21	12	24'	90	20
Imperial 24×42	6,500	21	12	25'3"	110	25
Imperial 32×50	7,300	21	12	26'	175	27
Cardwell Machinery, Richmond, Virginia						
22×28	NA	19	6	11'6"	NA	4
28×40	NA	19	6	12'	NA	6

Trade Name	Weight (lb)	Cylinder Diameter	No. of Bars	Separator Length	Capacity (bu./hr.)	HP Required
J. I. Case Co., Racine, Wisconsin						
20×28	NA	22	9	20'4"	100	20
22×36	NA	22	12	23'5"	200	25
28×46	NA	22	12	25'8"	275	34
32×54	NA	32	20	27'9"	300	50
Clark Machine Co., St. Johnsville, New York						
Williams 28×36	3,500	18	12	22'	100	12
Williams 26×38	5,000	22	12	23'	180	20
Williams 34×50	5,800	22	12	27'	300	30
Climax Corp., Batavia, New York						
Batavia 28×42	7,000	28	12	29'9"	140	25
Batavia 32×48	7,500	28	12	29'9"	160	35
Batavia 36×54	8,000	28	12	29'9"	180	40
Deere & Co., Moline, Illinois						
24×42	5,800	22	12	24'4"	200	25
28×50	6,300	22	12	24'4"	250	35
Doylestown Agricultural Co., Doylestown, Pennsylvania						
No. 2 26×33	2,500	19	9	16'	30	6
No. 3 26×37	2,700	19	9	16'	50	7
Jr. Stl. 26×34	3,000	21	9	20'	75	12
Dylstwn 22×34	3,950	21	12	21'	75	12
Ellis Keystone, Potstown, Pennsylvania						
Champion						
No. 1 O'shot 20×27	2,750	21	12	NA	40	12
No. 1 U'shot 19×46	2,850	21	12	19'7"	40	15
No. 2 U'shot 22×37	4,400	21	12	21'5"	90	20
28×46 Steel	3,800	21	12	21'5"	120	30
Frick Co., Waynesboro, Pennsylvania						
Model A 20×34	4,200	20	12	18'	120	22
Steel 22×36	5,000	20	12	23'6"	160	30
Steel 28×47	6,250	23	12	27'6"	250	45
28×48	6,900	23	12	25'	250	45
Geiser Mfg. Co., Waynesboro, Pennsylvania						
No. 4 25×32	4,600	18	9	18'6"	50	20
Peerless 25×37	6,900	21	12	21'	75	36
Peerless C1 30×45	8,000	21	12	23'2"	110	45
John Goodison, Sarnia, Ontario						
23×38	6,400	22	12	25'6"	160	22
25×42	7,550	22	12	29'6"	200	27
28×46	7,750	22	12	29'6"	230	35
36×50	8,700	22	12	30'6"	250	50
32×54	8,900	22	12	30'6"	275	50
Harrison Machine, Belleville, Illinois						
Belleville						
Baby 24×37	6,300	21	12	31'	80	20
Std. 28×41	6,800	21	12	31'	120	25
New Great Western						
28×53	8,200	26	15	31'6"	200	30
32×57	8,450	26	15	31'6"	220	36
36×61	8,750	26	15	31'6"	300	40

Trade Name	Weight (lb)	Cylinder Diameter	No. of Bars	Separator Length	Capacity (bu./hr.)	HP Required
Heebner & Sons, Lansdale, Pennsylvania						
Pennsylvania						
No. 3 21×28	2,060	26	9	NA	15	4
Little Giant						
No. 2 26×33	2,635	31	9	NA	30	6
No. 1 30×37	3,000	35	9	NA	40	8
Heebner Special						
U'shot 26×31	3,600	31	9	15'	35	10
Huber Mfg. Co., Marion, Ohio						
Supreme						
22×40	5,480	21	12	24'8"	200	25
28×46	6,200	21	12	26'4"	250	30
28×48	8,000	24	12	28'9"	300	35
32×54	8,800	24	12	28'9"	300	40
International Harvester Co., Chicago, Illinois						
McCormick-Deering						
22×38	5,200	21	12	23'	220	20
28×46	5,420	21	12	23'	280	30
Keck-Gonnerman Co., Vernon, Indiana						
Indiana Special						
Junior 21×38	5,400	22	12	24'9"	90	20
Junior 28×48	6,000	22	12	24'9"	165	30
Standard 32×54	9,000	28	15	28'5"	200	50
Standard 36×62	10,000	28	15	28'5"	250	70
Messinger Mfg., Tatamy, Pennsylvania						
Ideal						
No. 20 20×30	2,500	24	9	18'	35	12
No. 24 24×36	4,000	24	9	20'	60	18
MacDonald Thresher Co., Stratford, Ontario						
Decker Special						
28×46	6,000	22	12	NA	125	30
Decker 32×54	7,500	28	16	NA	175	40
Minneapolis-Moline, Minneapolis, Minnesota						
Twin City 21×36	4,620	23	9	26'5"	100	18
Minneapolis 22×36	5,700	22	12	23'4"		20
Twin City 28×46	6,500	24	12	29'	250	25
Minneapolis 28×46	7,040	22	12	28'	250	30
Twin City 28×48	7,850	22	12	29'6"	230	26
Minneapolis 36×58	9,720	28	16	30'8"		50
Minneapolis 40×64	9,990	28	16	30'8"		65
Twin City 32×52	10,360	28	15	33'6"	300	45
Oliver Farm Equip., Nichols & Shepard Division, Battle Creek, Michigan						
Red River Special						
22×36	5,600	22	12	23'6"	NA	25
22×46	6,680	22	12	25'6"	NA	35
32×56	9,150	28	16	27'	NA	50
Pioneer Thresher, Shortsville, New York						
Pioneer						
F-22×36	4,075	20	10	20'6"	110	18
#3 30×40	4,500	20	8	22'6"	130	20
#2 30×40	4,800	20	10	24'	150	25
O 32×47	6,000	22	12	26'	300	30
OO B 32×53	6,900	22	12	26'	350	35

Trade Name	Weight (lb)	Cylinder Diameter	No. of Bars	Separator Length	Capacity (bu./hr.)	HP Required
Port Huron, Port Huron, Michigan						
Tractor Special						
21 × 36, Steel	5,300	22	9Dbl	24'4"	150	18
25 × 40, Steel	5,550	22	9Dbl	24'4"	250	25
Sawyer-Massey, Hamilton, Ontario						
No. 1 22 × 36	6,570	22	12	23'9"	100	25
No. 1B 25 × 44	6,800	22	12	23'9"	150	30
No. 2B 29 × 48	7,070	22	12	23'9"	175	40
No. 3 33 × 56	8,300	22	12	25'7"	225	70
Waterloo Mfg., Waterloo, Ontario						
Waterloo						
Special 22 × 36	5,640	21	12	26'6"	75	17
Champion 24 × 36	6,620	21	12	26'6"	100	20
Champion 24 × 42	7,125	21	12	29'	125	24
Champion 28 × 48	7,350	21	12	29'	150	26
Champion 33 × 52	8,850	28	16	29'	200	40
Champion 36 × 56	9,120	28	16	29'	250	45
Geo. White & Sons, London, Ontario						
White						
22 × 40	6,500	22	12	25'	120	20
24 × 46	7,000	22	12	25'	130	25
28 × 50	7,500	22	12	25'	150	30
Wood Bros., Des Moines, Iowa						
21 × 36	5,350	25	12	27'6"	NA	20
26 × 46	5,750	25	12	27'6"	NA	25
28 × 46	5,850	25	12	27'6"	NA	28
30 × 50	6,225	25	12	27'6"	NA	30

Tractor and Thresher Clubs

Clubs and Newsletters

For a directory of Engine and Threshing Shows, Stemgas Publishing Company issues an annual directory. For a copy, contact:

PO Box 328
Lancaster, PA 17603

The directory lists shows in virtually every area of the country. Stemgas also publishes *Gas Engine Magazine* and *Iron-men Album,* magazines for the enthusiast.

Newsletters providing a wealth of information and lore about individual brands of antique farm tractors and equipment have been on the scene for some time. More are springing up each year, so the following list is far from complete.

Antique Power
Patrick Ertel, editor
PO Box 838
Yellow Springs, OH 45387

Green Magazine (John Deere)
R. & C. Hain, editors
RR 1
Bee, NE 68314

M-M Corresponder (Minneapolis-Moline)
Roger Mohr, editor
Rt 1, Box 153
Vail, IA 51465

The N-Newsletter
Gerard W. Rinaldi
PO Box 235
Chelsea, VT 05038-0235

Old Abe's News (Case)
David T. Erb, editor
Rt 2, Box 2427
Vinton, OH 45686

Old Allis News (Allis Chalmers)
Nan Jones, editor
10925 Love Rd.
Belleview, MI 49021

Oliver Collector's News
Dennis Gerszewski, editor
Rt 1
Manvel, ND 58256-0044

Prairie Gold Rush (Minneapolis-Moline)
R. Baumgartner, editor
Rt 1
Walnut, IL 61376

Red Power (International Harvester)
Daryl Miller, editor
Box 277
Battle Creek, IA 51006

Wild Harvest (Massey-Harris, Ferguson)
Keith Oltrogge, editor
1010 S Powell
Box 529
Denver, IA 50622

Threshing Shows

Fond memories of bygone days; days recreated for both the nostalgia of those who lived them and for those who were not yet born. That's what Engine and Threshing Shows are all about: Thresherees, as they are called today. Mostly, it's a time when old men, who have worked hard to make a living in their prime, can bask in the glory of those days, and, like the biblical oxen, take a bite of the grain.

Entertainment and History

For those who like their history entertaining, Engine and Threshing Shows are for you, regardless of whether you are a youngster, a woman, or a man. No matter who you are, there is always good food—and everyone enjoys that!

There are two ways to approach the Engine and Threshing Show scene: as a spectator or as a participant. You start at the first level and are drawn to the second.

Lois and Mike Kolb of Oshkosh, Wisconsin, are invited to thresherees all over the Midwest, to show their 5in-to-the-foot working scale model of a Case Model A thresher which Mike Kolb made. Mike also made a half-scale Rumely Oil-Pull 20-40, which he uses to drive the model thresher.

For the spectator, the excitement probably centers on the threshing demonstrations. There are usually two or three of the big machines, of various ages, to be demonstrated. Each, in turn, is belted to a steam or gas tractor; a wagonload of bundles is brought up, and before you know it, there is a small mountain of straw behind the thresher. At some shows, there is a competition between two teams of threshers to see which team can get its engine into position, belted up, and ready to go faster. Lining up a 20 ton steam engine when time is important can be an exasperating experience.

In addition to threshing demonstrations, you can count on seeing operating sawmills, shingle mills, corn choppers, fire wood saws, and old-time washing machines, each driven by an appropriate antique power unit, from steam to the tiny two-cylinder Maytag engine.

The food tents do their best to bring back the flavor of the thresher dinner. Usually, you have chicken and pork chops, potatoes, beans, applesauce, and pies and cakes. Hot coffee and iced tea are also available. For the less-hearty appetite, there are choices of hamburgers, hot dogs, and cold sandwiches.

Every afternoon, right after lunch, comes the big parade. There are usually grandstands for spectators and an announcer with a public address system to keep the spectators informed. Parades last over an hour at most shows, as each antique capable of propelling itself around the route is entered. Often, specific brands of tractors are featured, such as Massey Harris or John Deere.

Then, there is the inevitable flea market. Because of the large crowds drawn to these Engine and Threshing Shows, dealers give them priority over regular flea markets.

There are also collections of handicrafts and models of farm equipment, including operating steam engines with threshing machines; art; farm produce; and antiques.

You will also find raffles, steam plowing demonstrations, tractor dynamometer tests, and pedal-power tractor pulls for the kids.

To become a participant is ridiculously easy! Just volunteer to help. Actually, the first step is usually to join the local Engine and Threshing Club. Next, get an old tractor or antique engine. Old-timers say you need not have your antique restored; just bring it to the show. They say that driving

William N. Rumely, dean of American threshing machine manufacturers (as this ad claims), reorganized Illinois Thresher Company in 1917, calling it now, The Rumely Robbins Company. The company's combination thresher-huller was still called the "Scientific."

your old tractor in your first parade will make you feel like you are a real participant! For club members, there are additional activities. Oats and wheat are cut with an old-time binder several days before the show. A real thrill for antique tractor owners is to be asked to pull the binder. The bundles are shocked and loaded on waiting wagons. Of course, someone has to prepare the field and do the planting. Then, during the rest of the year, club members support other community activities, such as Lion's Club days, children's Christmas party parades, pumpkin festivals, and the like. Any profits in the club's treasury are used to pay for maintenance of club-owned machinery and buildings and to buy and restore more farm antiques.

One of the best farming museums in Canada is the Ontario Agricultural Museum in Milton, Ontario.

In Great Britain, two of the best museums and shows are the Somerset Rural Life Museum in Glastonbury, Somerset; and the Great Dorset Steam Fair near Blandford, Dorset. This event is held in the last week of August every year.

Sources and Recommended Reading

Sources and Recommended Reading

Many of the following books are available through Classic Motorbooks/Motorbooks International, PO Box 1, Osceola, WI 54020 or by calling 800-826-6600.

Farm Inventions by Paul C. Johnson. Wallace-Homestead Book Co., Des Moines, IA.

Old Farm Tools and Machinery by Percy W. Blandford. Gale Research Co., Ft. Lauderdale, FL.

Farm Machinery and Equipment by Harris Smith and Lambert Wilkes. McGraw-Hill Book Co., New York, NY.

American Farm Tools, Hand to Steam by D. R. Hurt. Sunflower Press.

American Agricultural Implements by Robert L. Audrey. Ayer Co. Publishing.

Implement and Tractor by Robert K. Mills. Intertec Publishing, Overland Park, KS.

Wheels of Farm Progress by Marvin McKinley. American Society of Agricultural Engineers.

Farm and Steam Shows, USA and Canada by Dana Close Jennings. North Plains Press.

The Grain Harvesters by Graeme Quick and Wesley Buchele. American Society of Agricultural Engineers.

Early Farm Life by Lise Gunby. Crabtree Publishing Co., Toronto, Ontario, and Chicago, Illinois.

The Allis Chalmers Story by C. H. Wendel. Crestline Publishing Co., Sarasota, FL.

150 Years of International Harvester by C. H. Wendel. Crestline Publishing, Sarasota, FL.

Harvest Triumphant by Merrill Denison. Wm. Collins Sons & Co. Ltd., London, Glascow, New York, Toronto, etc.

Minneapolis-Moline Tractors 1870-1969 by C. H. Wendel & Andrew Morland. Motorbooks International, Osceola, WI.

"The Threshing Saga" by David T. Erb. *Old Abe News.*

Ford Tractors by Robert N. Pripps and Andrew Morland. Motorbooks International, Osceola, WI.

The American Farm Tractor: A History of the Classic Tractor by Randy Leffingwell. Motorbooks International, Osceola, WI.

International McCormick Tractors by Henry Rasmussen. Motorbooks International, Osceola, WI.

John Deere Tractors by Henry Rasmussen. Motorbooks International, Osceola, WI.

Case Tractors by Dave Arnold. Motorbooks International, Osceola, WI.

How to Restore Your Farm Tractor by Robert N. Pripps. Motorbooks International, Osceola, WI.

Index